Tiny Hands in Unorganised Sector

Tiny Hands in Unorganised Sector

Towards Elimination of Child Labour

S.N. MISHRA

SWETA MISHRA

SHIPRA

ISBN: 81-7541-174-0

First Published in India in 2004

Tiny Hands in Unorganised Sector

Published by:
Shipra Publications
115-A Vikas Marg, Shakarpur,
Delhi-110092, India.
Tel.: 91-11-22458662, 22500954; Fax : 91-11-22458662
E-mail: info@shiprapublications.com
www.shiprapublications.com

Laser Typeset by:
Sunshine Graphics
Delhi-110032

Printed at:
Chaudhary Offset Process,
Delhi-110051

Preface

The problem of child labour in general and the problems of children working in the informal sector in particular, is quite thought provoking and needs special attention particularly when we have entered into the nuclear age. The term child labour is at times used as employed child or working child. In this sense it is co-extensive with any work done by a child for gain. It signifies employment of children in gainful occupations with a view to add to the household income. Child labour includes children who prematurely leading adult lives, working long hours for low wages under conditions damaging to their health and to their physical and mental development, sometimes separated from their families, frequently deprived of meaningful education and training opportunities that could open up for them a better future.

The lack of attention given to the problem of child labour in the past is the perceived difficulty of distinguishing between positive and negative child work. There are cultural, economic and educational reasons to support the widely held view that work can be positive for children. Through work children can gain increasing status as family members and citizens. They can learn the skills of their parents and neighbours. Work can therefore build their confidence and self esteem, and can be a painless and gradual initiation into adult life. However, the concept of child labour begins with the working child himself/herself who is often deprived of his childhood opportunities for alround personality development. The conflict between economic pursuits and those of growth and education give rise to the problem of child labour.

The present study concentrates on children working in all categories throughout the Delhi city and peculiar categories of children working in particular areas of Delhi City. We hope that the study will provide direction to policy makers, academics and future researchers. Thus the focus of the study is on providing the perspective on child labour in India and Delhi in particular, examining the reasons for emergence of child labourers, locating the various categories of work in which the children are engaged, examining the socio-economic profile of the child workers and finally, discussing the role of international organisations like ILO, UNICEF, etc. in combating the child labour.

During the completion of the study we received immense help and cooperation from various individuals and organisations. We shall be failing in our duties if we do not record our appreciation for them.

First and foremost thanks are due to our Director, Dr. P.L. Sanjeev Reddy, who always encouraged, motivated and helped in getting a small grant from the NCT of Delhi which helped us in completing the study. Any amount of praise and appreciation will be inadequate for the services and cooperation provided by him.

The government of NCT of Delhi, particularly the then Labour Commissioner, S.P. Marwah, IAS, is claimant of our thanks. But for his sincere efforts, we could not have received a grant of Rupees thirty-seven thousand five hundred. We are also thankful to the Additional Labour Commissioner and his staff for help and cooperation.

Our sincere thanks are due to the respondent child workers who inspite of the scolding of their masters helped cooperate in answering the pointed query of ours. But for their cooperation this study would have been a dream unfulfilled.

Last but not the least, our sincere thanks are due to Shri H.P. Singh, who typed the odd pages of manuscript with keen interest and sincerity, which helped a lot in submitting the report within the record time.

Contents

List of Tables

List of Abbreviations

AMIC	Action Against the Most Intolerable
BBA	Bachpan Bachao Andolan
CAPART	Council for Advancement of People and Rural Technology
CLASP	Child Labour Action Support Programme
CREDA	Centre for Rural Education and Development Action
CRY	Child Relief and You
DCCW	Delhi Council for Child Welfare
DDP	Desert Development Programme
DJP	Development, Justice and Peace
DPAP	Drought Prone Area Programme
DPEP	District Primary Education Programme
DRDA	District Rural Development Agency
DWCRA	Development of Women and Children in Rural Areas
EAS	Employment Assurance Scheme
ICCW	Indian Council for Child Welfare
ICDS	Integrated Child Development Scheme
ILO	International Labour Organization
IPEC	International Programme on the Elimination of Child Labour
IRDP	Integrated Rural Development Programme
ISBT	Inter State Bus Terminus
JRY	Jawahar Rojgar Yojana
NAECL	National Authority for Elimination of Child Labour
NCLP	National Child Labour Project
NCT	National Capital Territory
NDMC	New Delhi Municipal Corporation
NFE	Non Formal Education
NGOs	Non Governmental Organizations
NIRD	National Institute of Rural Development

NLM	National Literacy Mission
NRCCL	National Resource Centre on Child Labour
ORG	Operations Research Group
PBG	Prayas Bal Grih
PCHB	Prayas Children's Home for Boys
PMRY	Prime Minister Rojgar Yojana
PROBE	Public Report on Basic Education in India
PSC	Programme Steering Committee
SACCS	South Asian Coalition on Child Servitude
SBT	Salam Balak Trust
SC	Scheduled Caste
SEWA	Self-Employed Women's Association
SIDA	State Industrial Development Agency
ST	Scheduled Tribe
TLC	Total Literacy Campaign
TRYSEM	Training for Rural Youth and Self Employment
UEE	Universal Elementary Education
UN	United Nations
UNDP	United Nations Development Programme
UNESCO	United Nations Educational Scientific and Cultural Organisation
UNICEF	United Nations Children's Fund
UPE	Universal Primary Education

1

Introduction

India faces a plethora of problems at the threshold of the 21st century. The problem of child labour in general and the problems of children working in the informal sector in particular, is quite thought — provoking and needs special attention particularly when we have entered into the nuclear age. It is one of the most important issues currently confronting the world. Inspite of growing awareness and concern for the problem, trends indicate that the number of children involved in child labour in certain sectors or in terms of geographical areas is increasing. If we really want to address the problem of child labour, it is all imperative that it is clearly defined and the whole concept is understood.[1]

But before entering into that exercise, it is necessary to know who is a child? A child, according to Article 24 of the Constitution of India and the child labour (Prohibition and Regulation) Act of 1986, is a person below the age of 14 years. The commonly accepted definition of a child in India is a person between 0 and 14 years of age.[2]

Maria De La Luz Silva defines a "child" as "some one who needs adult protection for physical, psychological and intellectual development until able to become independently integrated into the adult world."[3]

Work

Work is a process intrinsic to life at all levels. Any process aimed at bridging the gap between needs originating in an organism and resources in the organism's environment satisfying those needs may be termed "Work". Therefore, work is a natural process. Work insures survival and to cease to work is to cease to life. It is a critical process to human existence and thus has serious implications to the development of self-image, self-esteem and identity. It is a crucial ingredient of social relations, self-discovery, self-expression and self-realization.[4] Work has a central role to play in one's lives as individuals and members of society. It is not only a source of goods and services which are essential for human survival, but also satisfies the important human needs of status and function which gives a person a sense of self-worth and enables him to relate meaningfully to others.

The definition of work would obviously differ from culture to culture and perhaps even from person to person. The Census of India defines work "as participation in any economically productive activity. Such participation may be physical or mental in nature. Work involves not only active work but also effective supervision and direction of work".[5] Fox and Herse-Biber have described it as any activity or expenditure of energy that produces services and products of value to other people. Richard Hall states that, "work is the effort or activity of an individual performed for the purpose of providing goods and services of value to others. It is also considered to be worthwhile for the individual to be so involved". Both these definitions limit the concept of work to productive economic activity only. While there is no doubt that these two definitions do cover a wide range, there are several activities which are not strictly economic, yet may be perceived as work.[6] A more appropriate definition of work could, therefore, be as follows:

Thus, work is purposeful activity involving the time and effort of a person generally performed to meet the expectations, specifications, requirements or needs of others or one's own, usually to obtain an exchange value, a recognition or personal satisfaction and perceived by the person concerned as work.

Labour

When children are engaged in the production process, not primarily to meet their physiological and psychological needs, but to meet the profit — motivated needs of the employer, the process they are engaged in may be called "labour."[7]

Labour in the broad sense of the term may be defined as 'any hand or brain work'. Labour, according to Prof. S.E. Thomas[8], "consists of all human effort of body or mind, which is undertaken in expectation or reward". In the view of Prof. Jevons[9], labour is any exertion of mind and body undertaken partly or wholly with a view to do some good, other than the pleasure derived directly from the work.

Distinction Between Work and Labour

Differentiating work and labour is determined by the particular social context, the quality of the various interactions and dynamics present in the production process. Both labour and work are born out of the ubiquitous human need to survive and much of the ambiguity that exists centers around this commonality. Those elements that make labour and work apparently synonymous are:

i) Both work and labour are organised human responses to design ways of securing resources and satisfying human needs for sustenance.
ii) These processes involve an exchange between human beings and the "natural" world.
iii) Both work and labour require human effort — an exercise of body and mind.

The distinction between work and labour is to be found in a critical overview of the climate in which these processes operate and the quality of the relationships in operation. Historically, socio-political, scientific and technological developments have led to a radical transformation of work into labour.[10] However, the yardstick should be that child work should be in the best interests of the child as the line differentiating child work and child labour is a thin one.

Child Work and Child Labour

It has been observed that not all work is harmful to children. Some work activities, provide practical knowledge and skills, and reinforce self-esteem among children. The distinction made between activities that are harmless or sometimes even beneficial, and work that is exploitative is useful as it makes it possible to set priorities in the battle against child labour.

A large number of children, the girls, in particular, make significant contributions to household maintenance including collecting fire-wood and water, looking after the younger siblings, looking after cattle and sheep, and even helping in agricultural activities. Yet another group of children may be encouraged to learn family arts and crafts as well as skills. In the urban sector, they work in a wide variety of activities from organized factories to roadside cafes, motor repairing workshops, street vending, shoe-shining, selling of newspapers, fruits and peanuts, domestic help in homes and even in organized beggary. When the adult roles are learnt slowly and smoothly in childhood, under the protection and supervision of parents or guardians the work is considered as a part of their socialization process. But when the work is imposed upon the child against his/her wishes at the cost of learning and play, which are necessary for the full development of his/her personality it becomes exploitative in nature and can be considered as labour. This work includes the participation of these children in the production of economic goods and services, including unpaid family work as well as work for pay or profit.[11]

Concept of Child Labour

The term "child labour" is, at times, used as "employed child" or "working child". In this sense it is co-extensive with any work done by a child for gain. It signifies employment of children in gainful occupations with a view to add to the household income. Moreover, children spend much of their time in household maintenance activities. In the definition of 'child labour', according to 1971 and 1981 census of India, "the stress was on the concept of main activity i.e. on the economically productive pursuits in which worker engaged himself or herself for most part of the time. As for seasonal work such as agriculture and ancillary pursuits, the main activity of a person was defined with reference to his or her work during the year preceding the enumeration. Further, if a person participated in economically productive work, not as a main activity or for most part of the year, he/she is not treated as worker but as marginal worker".

The use of the concept "exploitation" for identifying child labour creates practical problems because 'exploitation' as a concept cannot be given a precise objective meaning. This lies in the eyes of the investigator. The investigator can only identify the extreme limits of work done by children. Thus, child labour is a part of child work which implies that all child labour can be termed as child work but not the other way round.

For the purpose of this study, children who are not in school, but are engaged in work have been divided into the following categories:

i) *Child labour*: It refers to those children who are doing paid work in workshops, establishments and in service sector such as domestic workers.
ii) *Street children*: It refers to children working in road-side and streets as rag-pickers. They are always found on the pavement, dhabas etc.
iii) *Working children*: It refers to those children who work as part of family labour and house-hold based work such as flower tying and selling etc.

The wide variation in the number of children reported to be working in different countries according to governments and different groups is related to the force with which one defines the concept. Some of the definitions on child labour are as follows:

The Encyclopaedia of social sciences defines child labour as: "When the business of wage earning or of participation in self or family support conflicts directly or indirectly with the business of growth and education, the result is child labour. The function of work in childhood is primarily developmental and not economic".

Homer Folks defines child labour as "...any work by children that interferes with their full physical development, their opportunities for a desirable minimum of education or their needed recreation."[12]

The International Labour Organisation (1983) defines child labour as follows: "child labour includes children prematurely leading adult lives, working long hours for low wages under conditions damaging to the health and to their physical and mental development, sometimes separated from the families, frequently deprived of meaningful education and training opportunities that would open up for them a better future".

According to Operations Research Group (ORG), "A working child is that child who was enumerated during the survey as a child falling within the 5-15 age bracket and who is at remunerative work may be paid or unpaid, within or outside the family."[13]

In some societies, age may not be a sufficient basis for defining "childhood". The fulfillment of certain social rites and traditional obligations may be an important requirement in defining "adult" and "child" status. In still others, the integration of children into socio-economic life may begin so early and the transition from childhood to adulthood may be so smooth and gradual, that it may be virtually impossible to identify clearly the different life phases. It can be recognized that, they are dealing with a concept which could mean different things depending on the context.[14]

The lack of attention given to the problem of child labour in the past is the perceived difficulty of distinguishing between positive and negative child work. There are cultural, economic and educational reasons to support the widely held view that work can be positive for children. Through work children can gain increasing status as family members and citizens. They can learn the skills of their parents and neighbours. Work can therefore build their confidence and self-esteem, and can be a painless and gradual initiation into adult life. In practice, many children work from an early age of 6 or 7, often on a family farm. Work can clearly be a positive influence on child development. Inspite of all these positive aspects, child labour is often seen as negative because, the problem is that when the conditions of work change, the picture changes dramatically. Work turns into exploitation when children:[15]

- *Work when they are too young*: Many children start factory work at 6 or 7 years for e.g., in the carpet industry.
- *Work too long hours*: In some cases 12-16 hours a day.
- *Work for very minimal returns*: as low as Rs. 120 for a 60 hour week or no pay, as in agriculture.
- *Work in hazardous conditions*: in mines, quarries, plantations, sweat shops or even on the streets.
- *Work under slave-like arrangements*: there are an estimated 20 million child bonded labourers in South Asia.

The Concept of Child in Relation to Labour

The concept of child labour begins with the working child himself/ herself who is often deprived of his childhood opportunities for all round personality development. The conflict between economic pursuits and those of growth and education give rise to the problem of child labour.

According to V.V. Giri, the term child labour is commonly interpreted in two different ways: First, as an economic practice and secondly, as a social evil. In the economic sense, it signifies employment of children in gainful occupations with a view to adding to the income of the family. It is in the social context that the term child labour is now more generally used.[16] In the social context, it takes into account the damages to which children are exposed, which means the denial of opportunities for development.[17] Technological progress widens the gap between family's ability to educate and the requirements of the productive system.[18]

Since the terms "Child" and "Labour" has been interpreted in various ways, the following definition has been adopted for the study.

The child is any person below the age of 14 years. Child labour is that form of work a child is engaged in, which is hazardous and harmful to the growth and development of the child. A child employed for others or self-employed contributing to family enterprise, domestic work, cultivation or who work as apprentices acquiring skills on the job would also be considered as child labour.

Children Working on the Street

These children are different from the other categories of urban child labour because of the different dimensions of their problems and their perceptions of life, lack of basic facilities of life, hazardous working conditions, nature of the world in which they live, unprotected and exploitative work they perform, psychological strain they undergo, their deprivation of parental love and affection, and above all, their negative attitude towards their own life and the society in which they live.[19] The term "Street Children" was coined sometime in the 1980's as a definite term, to identify children who have chosen to spend most of their time on the streets in various occupations.

UNICEF suggested that the term "Street children" refer to children who work on the streets of urban areas, without reference to the time they spend there or to reason for being there. There are no statistical estimates of the total population of street children. But UNICEF has put the global figure as 30 million.

The term "street children" not only denotes a place of congregation, but also a certain set of working and living conditions. The very fact that they are in the street means that, most of them face some common but difficult situations. The vast majority of children are in the street to make a living for their families or themselves. The return may be paltry and may be in kind rather than in cash, but to these children the street is above all a work place. They spend large amount of time in the street, chiefly because of the low returns on their labour. Most of them make their way in the informal sector as petty hawkers, shoe-shine boys, rag-pickers and sometimes petty pick-pockets and even drug pedlars. By nature of their work and life, they are normally on their own, largely unprotected by adults.[20] All street children are necessarily working children, though not all working children are street children.[21]

While discussing the labour situation, a distinction has been made about those children 'on the streets' and those 'of the streets'. "Children on the streets" are seen as "marketable" children, engaging in work to supplement family income or as part of family labour. This refers to those children who maintain regular contact with their family, but spend a majority of their time working on the streets. "Children of the street" refers to those ;who actually live and work on the streets. Children who have left their homes and have no family contacts are forced to work to support themselves. Work for them symbolizes their autonomy and independence. They control the income they earn. Lack of opportunities for saving leads to children spending almost all their earned money on food, snacks and movies thus depicting an integral aspect of street culture. While the former represents 'forced labour', the latter stems out of a necessity. Living in a "street culture" influenced by deviant behaviour of anti-social elements pose a threat to the emotional and mental well-being of street children. Longing for the warmth of a family who abandoned them or whom they have known, hungry for the love of a mother, these children may grow up with a warped sense of reality.

There are several forms of child labour throughout India. Children are found in the urban and rural labour force in what is called the "informal sector". The terms, 'unorganised sector' and 'informal sector' have been used synonymously in the study.

Informal sector is a manifestation of urban poverty and low

levels of income of a majority of urban population. In Delhi, earlier estimates had indicated that the unorganized sector accounts for as much as 50 per cent to 70 per cent of employment.

There is no consensus of opinion of what is meant by the informal sector. It has been defined in terms of several parameters. The most simple one is to consider it to be that component of the economy which is not included in the formal or organized sector, in the sense, that it is not regulated by, or subject to, all specific rules and regulations that normally apply to units engaged in economic activities in the organized or formal sector. The most common parameter used to define the informal sector is the number of workers, generally less than a specified figure, which ranges between 5 and 25.[22]

The informal sector comprises mostly of small-scale units, largely of individuals, self-employed producers in urban areas. They are informal in the sense that, they are for the most part unregistered and unrecorded in official statistics/studies. They generally confine the employment to the members of their families. A few would hire workers. They use very little capital and a low level of technology and skills. Productivity is generally low. Incomes are irregular and employment is highly unstable. The informal sector has tended to respond rather than to lead. It has responded to the growth of incomes in agriculture and in urban activities, but has in turn added to the growth of consumer expenditure.

Informal sector includes not only traditional artisans, services and petty traders but also small units in manufacturing, construction, trade and commerce, transport and service sectors engaged in the production of goods and services (with sole proprietorship or engaging more persons) which operate on a very small-scale and have no formal business organization. Thus, the various elements of the definition of the informal sector indicate a broad spectrum of urban poor households which are heterogenous ranging from employment in small-scale industries to self-employment, skilled and unskilled, including street vendors and petty traders with low and irregular income.[23]

In India, the informal sector is multi-dimensional with urban and rural complexes of related occupations that overlap to some degree. In urban areas, the informal sector embraces a variety of commercial, transportation, repair and productive activities. In rural areas, though traditional village crafts and household industries are important sources for informal sector work, commercial, transport and repair activities are not uncommon.

Keith Hart, who gave initial currency to the concept of informal sector distinguished formal from informal sectors income opportunities.[24] In contrast to the formal sector the latter comprises of all non-wage sources of income, whether legitimate or illegitimate. This distinction is essentially based on wage earning and self-employment.[25]

Focusing on the employment and development policies in an urban economy, informal sector is defined as one which "consists of small-scale units engaged in the production and distribution of goods and services with the primary objectives of generating employment and income to their participants notwithstanding the constraints on capital both physical and human.[26]

The "informal sector" is looked upon by many as a sort of sewer in the economy, collecting all the drop-outs, all those who failed to make good and thus act as an obstacle on economic progress in any programme for modernization.[27] As a result of such an attitude, there is a tendency among statisticians and surveyors to overlook enumeration of labour force participation in this sector. Most surveys cover a major part of wage-earning employment and some self-employment in the larger and more organized firms, but neglect a range of wage earners and self-employed persons, including many children in the informal sector. In fact, the unorganized nature of the sector makes it difficult to assess the nature of employment in this sector.[28]

Factors Responsible for Employment of Children in the Informal Sector

There are certain factors which enable children to seek employment in the informal sector. these factors include:[29]

i) absence of any statutory minimum age for employment;
ii) easy entry and easy exist;
iii) less competition among job seekers;
iv) absence of any minimum requirement of education or training;
v) easy nature of work;
vi) provision of food, shelter and clothing in the city by the employer; and
vii) absence of any minimum wage requirements.

These factors enable the child labour to enter the informal sector as and when they like. Broadly speaking, four types of children are found engaged in the informal sector. They are: children belonging to poor families undertaking jobs to supplement their parents income; children who have none to support them; children who are sent to urban areas by their parents in rural areas for earning a living and children who run away from their families.

Absence of a Suitable Protective and Regulative Labour Legislation

The emergence of urban informal sector as a major source of employment and income in the Third World countries in recent years is primarily a manifestation of increasing pressure of population growth juxtaposed against the inadequate growth of employment and income opportunities in rural areas and small urban centers on the one hand, and in the formal and government sectors of the urban economy on the other. Rising inflation rate and growing poverty further aggravate the situation and force a number of children to enter into the informal sector for a living.

A large percentage of children start working because of being orphaned, rejected by parents or because of broken families and other.domestic problems. These children go into the streets totally abandoned with no one to care for them.

The number of children who enter in the informal sector in cities like Calcutta, New Delhi, Chennai, Mumbai, Kanpur, Bangalore, Ahmedabad, Patna have increased in the recent years. Although the central government and various State Governments are aware of the situation and the exploitation of the child labour in the informal sector, no significant effort has been made so far to adopt a comprehensive legislation regulating the employment conditions of child labour in the informal sector. Unless a comprehensive legislation or a legislation of composite nature dealing with wages, hours of work, health, safety, welfare facilities, leave and holiday, social security, retrenchment, dismissal and discharge is adopted, and a suitable enforcement machinery is created for this purpose, nothing tangible can be achieved.

Although it is not easy to have proper enforcement of any legislation in the informal sector, initiatives must be taken. Factors like scattered nature of undertakings, lack of records or proper information, absence of unionism, absence of formal employer-employee relationship, illiteracy and ignorance among children, inadequacy of the enforcement machinery, are some of the factors responsible for lack of a suitable labour legislation in the country dealing with child labour in the informal sector.[30]

There are five categories of children who could be brought within the ambit of child labour, even if such categories may not fall within the ambit of the definition of child labour (Prohibition and Regulation) Act 1986. They participate in various capacities throughout the informal sector such as:[31]

- Children who are self-employed;
- Wage earners paid by the hour or for piece labour;
- Apprentices employed in order that a skill will eventually be mastered;
- Children who assist an adult who is accountable to an employer; and
- Children who co-produce with their family without any direct remuneration.

Despite their gigantic numbers, they have been by-passed by protective legislation. The Indian Constitution is eloquent on the recognition of dignity and worth of human life including the tender life of a child and the need for its protection. This is clear from the provisions mentioned in Articles 21, 24, 39 and 41.

India has probably the largest child labour force in the world and it is growing every day despite increasing concern at local, national and international levels. It is estimated that 100 million children[32] are forced to work in organized and unorganized sectors. It is further estimated that 133 million children are not attending schools for various reasons. But every estimate of child labour falls far short of the reality owing to the number of procedures and other general limitations. However, in stark reality, all surveys and studies shows that the child labour is rampant where there is more number of illiterates. The existence of child labour in whatever form and magnitude should be a matter of concern to the parents, society and State.

The specific provisions enshrined in the chapter on Directive Principles of State Policy and the Fundamental Rights of the Constitution of India[33] provide legal protection to child labourers from exploitation at work. But it was only in 1985 that the problem of child labour entered the public consciousness with some persistence. The debate on this subject was initiated when Government announced its intention in 1985 to introduce fresh legislation to deal with the phenomenon of child labour. However, no concerted efforts were made at the national level to withdraw children from hazardous employment, except a Comprehensive National Child Labour Policy, which provides a broad framework for tackling the issue of child labour through legislative action plan, general programmes and project — oriented action plans in areas prone to child labour. A Child Labour Technical Advisory Committee which was responsible to co-ordinate and intensify ongoing development programmes for income generation and employment in child labour concentration areas was constituted. Nevertheless, working children in the urban unorganized sector remain largely unseen and therefore overlooked by law, policy and developmental intervensions.

To supplement the governmental initiatives at the national level, international donor agencies came forward to support two parallel programmes in 1992 (i) the Child Labour Action Support Programme (CLASP) and (ii) International Programme on the Elimination of Child Labour (IPEC).

It was hoped that these programmes would build the capacity of government and non-governmental agencies and the human resource development of their functionaries. The International Labour Organisation implements these programmes under the overall guidance and supervision of National Level Steering Committees headed by the Union Labour Secretary. The Steering Committees have representatives of Government and non-governmental organization. India is one of the first among countries to join the IPEC which is under implementation in several other countries. The long term objective of IPEC is to contribute towards abolition of child labour. The IPEC in India is the largest in the world and has led to action programmes benefitting about one lakh child labourers.

UNICEF acknowledges the need to seriously address child labour as a key component of the organization's policy to advocate the implementation of the convention on the Rights of the child and the achivement of goals for improving the conditions and well being of children. UNICEF has been funding government and non-governmental organisations including National Resource Centre on Child Labour for elimination of child labour in India.

The working children constitute a heterogenous group in terms of their socio-economic background, age, skills, attitudes and approach to life, preferences and needs. In Delhi, all working children are not totally illiterate. Some are semi-literate while few others are drop-outs and few have relapsed back into the world of illiteracy and have outlived their literacy skills. Some have reached upto class 4 or 5. Some of them are exceptionally bright and intelligent and in terms of such natural endowment may even be superior to the normal children. Some of them are good orators and have exceptional qualities. So, it is difficult to put all such children in the same pattern of education, regardless of variations in their skills and experiences.

This study concentrates on a special category of children, namely child workers in the Informal sector. Besides this, strategies adopted by the Government and non-governmental organizations like non-formal education, skill training, health care, rehabilitation measures, advocacy have been touched upon to an extent in this study.

Overview of Literature

Various studies on child labour have been conducted since 1979, either at the national level, regional level or industry wise. The educational institutions, government and non-governmental organizations have undertaken projects on child labour. Looking at child labour as a multi-dimensional social problem which no single approach can catch-hold, various scholars, planners, researchers and technocrats have analysed it from different angles.

Jinesh Chandra Kulshreshtra's[34] study, Child Labour in India, brings forth some vital aspects of child labour and its evil consequences. It reveals that large families, poverty, ignorance of parents, absence of family allowances and compulsory education are the root cause for the prevalence of child labour in India. Besides, inadequate legislation coupled with its inefficient enforcement are also responsible for the continuation of child labour.

Mohd. Mustafa and Onkar Sharma in their study, Child Labour in India — A Bitter Truth[35], deal with working conditions of child labour in Delhi covering working children in six vocations: tea stalls, dhabas, automobile workshops, domestic child workers — other three of self-employed: shoe-shining, rag picking, evening newspaper hawkers. It reviews the various child labour legislations as also some selected Supreme Court Judgements regarding child labour. The study of Neera Burra[36] Born to Work, concentrates on the working children of specific industries of glass making, brassware, gem polishing and lock making. She describes the socio-economic conditions of the child labourers and hazardous processes involved in the work. The study brings to light the fact that a large number of children as young as five or six years work through the night under great health and safety hazards resulting in stunting the growth of these children both mentally and physically. Even the state policies aimed at protecting children are poorly conceived and badly enforced. B.K. Sharma and Vishwa Mittar's[37] Child Labour and Urban Informal Sector highlights the significant role that the urban informal sector has come to play in providing employment to child labourers in a developing economy. The socio-economic structure, the family base, the level of income and employment, the occupational mobility and the contribution of child labour towards family income are some of the other aspects analysed in the study.

Pramila H. Bhargava's work, The Elimination of Child Labour: Whose Responsibility,[38] is a compilation of her field notes and experiences which gives a true picture of the child labour problem. It narrates the work done in an area which is drought prone, dominated by extremists, very backward and where incidence of rural child labour is very high. It focuses on the need for the convergence of various departments and ministries as a pre-requisite for the elimination of child labour.

Lakshmidhar Mishra's study Child Labour in India[39] analyses the oppressive reality of Indian Labouring children and provides perhaps the fullest macro-perspective on the nature and scale of the problem, as well as what this problem means in human and economic terms. The author critically examines constitutional and legal provisions on the subject, the national policy and programme action, international instruments and recent international initiatives, and the role of NGOs, trade unions, central employers organizations, and the media. Mendelievich's[40] Children at Work states that the reason for employing children has been to supplement the family income, when it has not been sufficient to meet the requirements of the family; and secondly, having more children is considered a great advantage, because every child means two extra hands to work, which means more income for the family.

A.N. Singh's[41] The Child Rag-pickers Socio-Economic Perspectives and Intervention Strategies, is a multi-disciplinary investigation into various aspects of pressing socio-economic problems facing child rag-pickers in slum areas of Kurukshetra, Haryana. The study provides a comprehensive evaluation of children's participation at work in general and rag-picking in particular. A similar study by A.N. Singh[42], Child Labour in India, Socio-Economic Perspective, reveals that economic conditions of majority of child workers families forced them to undertake carpet weaving.

Richard Anker et al in their study Economics of Child Labour in Hazardous Industries of India[43], which is a collection of papers addressing the problem of child labour, presents the findings of studies based on child labour in carpet, glass, diamond and gem industries. It gives an understanding on the economics of replacing child labour with adult labour in these industries. The study further highlighted that non pecuniary and non economical factors are often very important reasons why employers hire children. The authors conclude that the elimination of child labour would cause only a small increase in the cost of production almost always below five per cent. It is also likely to increase the prevailing wage rate because of a reduction in the supply of labour.

Child Labour in India[44], an empirical study of Orissa, by S.K. Tripathy, looks into the causes, magnitude and extent of the problem in our country. The work analyses the safeguards presently available at international and national level, the ILO's work in this area and relevant national legislations, available in the past and present, along with their overall implementation in the present context. Finally, the author suggests possible measures, for the rehabilitation of these children and gradual removal of the problem.

Myron Weiner's[45] study, The Child and the State in India, provides a brief picture of the situation of India's children: their place in the labour force and in the school system. The book presents a descriptive analysis of the attitudes of government officials, educators and activists toward child labour and shows how these attitudes shape Indian policies toward compulsory education and child labour laws. Finally, the author examines the experiences of South Korea, Taiwan, the People's Republic of China, Sri Lanka and several other contemporary instances in the third world where states have successfully intervened to enforce compulsory education and markedly brought down the incidence of child labour.

B.N. Shukla and Bimla Shukla[46] in their theoretical study on Child Labour in the Informal Sector touches upon certain questions like the nature and composition of the child labour force, factors that bring them in to informal sector, their wages and conditions of employment and causes for the apathy on the part of the government for not undertaking any significant ameliorative steps.

Working Children in Urban India by B.R. Patil[47], is a comprehensive survey which attempts to analyse the problem of child labour at the macro level with reference to India as also the reasons why the children have taken to wage labour. It also brings out the harsh realities of child employment with regard to their wages and monthly earnings/income and reveals that the meagre wages the children earn is the means of survival for their families. Finally, it outlines some policy measures to tackle the problem of child labour in the short term and its elimination in the long run. I.S. Singh's study on Child Labour[48] focuses on the incidence of child labour, socio-economic background of the child labourers, types of services and areas where there is concentration of child labour and the age group so employed. It examines the child labourers mental capacities with special instruments and compares mental abilities of the child labourers engaged in different services with those of normal children of the same age group.

S.N. Tripathy's work on Exploitation of Child Labour in Tribal India[49], analyses the multi-dimensional problem of child labour, causes of child labour and its magnitude, as demonstrated in India, from a historical perspective. It explores the socio-economic and historical factors responsible for child labour in Orissa and particularly in the tribal and backward district of Phulbani. Besides this, it analyses the features of the problem of child labour manifested in the tribal district of Phulbani. Finally, it examines the various legislations enacted both by the central and state governments which aims at removing the exploitation of the child labourers.

Nadeen Mohsin in his paper on "Poverty: Breeding ground for Child Labour"[50] has described the historical development of child labour and the legislative facilities for child labour. It was found that acute poverty was the main reason forcing children to seek jobs. The author suggested adopting a two-sided approach to the problem — one that eliminates household poverty, and the other, that makes education compulsory for all children. The former would come through improved employment and wages and better conditions of work for the householders, and the latter through incentives in the form of free books, food, clothes, medicines etc. to all school-going children.

V. Verma in his paper on "Child Labour Need for Social Awareness"[51] emphasises for a plan of action in the field, removal of barriers of ignorance and backwardness; and the need for a specific thrust on education. No dramatic result can be expected and without people's participation and social awareness, the flow of child labour cannot be diverted.

G.K. Murthy and T.J. Rani,[52] in their paper on "Wages of Child Labour", have examined the pattern of wages of child labour in small restaurants in the context of the minimum wages prescribed by the state government. It also analyses the socio-economic variables that motivate the employers to engage and the employees to get into service. Finally, the paper examines the importance of certain factors viz., nature of work, capacity of the employer to pay, the hours of work, ethical considerations, levels of income, etc., on wage determination.

Most of the studies reviewed so far, revealed that no study has been taken up on child labour in informal sector of Delhi City except few categories on rag-pickers, sundae vendors and domestic workers. The present study concentrates on children working in all categories throughout the Delhi City and peculiar categories of children working in particular areas of Delhi City. The study would help to provide direction to policy makers, legal experts and future researchers, since there is hardly any background information to get started on how to bring them under legal framework and provide better amenities, wages and safeguard their individuality in the informal sector.

Purpose of the Study

The problem of child labour has entered the public consciousness only during the recent years. Since then, an increasing number of individuals and organizations have been involved with making films, audio visuals, researching different areas where child labour is widely prevalent, writing in the press and holding seminars in an attempt to comprehend the problem.

But so far, to our knowledge, no significant research work has focused on child labour in informal sector and various categories of work done by children in Delhi. The present study is basically an attempt to fill up this gap. The study also concentrates on the peculiar categories of work done by children who are not covered by legislation. Further, media reports and UNICEF'S statements on the probable eradication of child labour prompted the researchers to take up the study.

Objectives of the Study

The objectives of the study are as follows:

1. To study the perspective of child labour in India and Delhi in particular;
2. To find out the various reasons for the emergence of child labourers in Delhi;
3. To locate the different categories of work in which children are employed in the informal sector of Delhi and their attitude towards work and education;
4. To study the socio-economic characteristics and family background of child workers in informal sector of Delhi;
5. To examine the role of International organizations i.e. ILO and UNICEF in combating child labour; and
6. Finally, to analyse the role of Government and Non-governmental organizations in ameliorating the condition of child workers.

Hypotheses

On the basis of earlier studies, personal observations, available reports and discussions on child workers, certain hypotheses were framed. These hypotheses are as follows:

Child labour cannot be eradicated because:

1. Family environment is the main cause for child labour (family environment refers to broken families, alcoholic

parents, lack of parental care and other undesirable habits among family members).

2. Illiteracy and low educational level of parents is an important factor for prevalence of child labour.
3. Poverty is one of the reason and not the only reason for the cause of child labour.
4. Most of the child labourers either have low or no interest in studies.
5. Most of the child labourers in Delhi are satisfied with their work.

Methodology

This is a descriptive cum analytical study. It portrays the problems and socio-economic characteristics of children working in Delhi and tries to provide solutions. A survey based on a sample of 250 child workers was conducted in the informal sectors of Delhi.

Both primary and secondary sources of information have been made use of in the study. Primary data for all categories of child workers were collected through personal interview using interview schedule. Besides, relevant data were also collected from published documents, policy-notes, reports and interactions with government officials and agency staff of non-governmental organizations. The secondary sources of data were collected from books, periodicals, journals and news papers available with the libraries.

As regards the sample method, we adopted random sampling. 250 working children were selected from different areas randomly and interviewed. Since they did not know English, we used to explain them in Hindi and their responses were noted down in the proper column of the questionnaire.

Different tools of empirical research viz., interview with child labourers with the help of structured and guided schedule, formal and informal discussions and participant observations etc. form part of the methodology of the present study. A field diary had also been maintained to note down the off-coming comments for analysis. The data and information so collected have been tabulated, analysed and presented in a report form.

Of the various methods of collecting data, direct personal interview method was found to be the most appropriate one in having interaction with the government and non-governmental organization officials. As majority of the child labourers were illiterate and many of them were school drop-outs, interview method gave an opportunity to observe their individual attitude and behaviour.

Aspects of the Study

The report has been coached in altogether seven chapters. As usual, the introductory chapter provides a brief account of the research problem in hand, the objectives of the study, the conceptual framework, hypothesis, universe of the study and methodology adopted.

The second chapter provides a detailed account of child labour in India. It focuses on the statistical details regarding child labour, the origin of child labour, the constitutional provisions related to child labour and the legal protection of children at work. Finally, the chapter discuses the factors responsible for child labour and problems of working children in India.

In the third chapter an attempt has been made to give an account of ILO's and UNICEF's concern for the child. It discusses the various conventions of ILO as also the ILO activities to combat child labour. Finally, an attempt is made to discuss the concern of UNICEF towards child labour.

The fourth chapter attempts to analyse the Government and NGO's concern for child labour. The chapter focusses on the work done by some NGOs with regard to elimination of child labour. The chapter suggests that a single individual or a group or one agency alone cannot solve the problem of child labour. It requires a multi pronged approach.

The fifth chapter presents a theoretical account of child labour in Delhi. An attempt has been made in the chapter to examine the types of working children, their occupation, the problems they are facing and the areas in which they are concentrated. Finally, an attempt has been made to analyse the role of NGOs which are engaged in elimination of child labour in the NCT of Delhi.

Sixth chapter provides the empirical view of the problem. In this chapter an attempt has been made to evaluate the perception of working children with regard to child labour. It focusses on the employment of child workers in the informal sector of Delhi and their socio economic characteristics viz., occupation, income, education, housing and working conditions.

The seventh and the final chapter is devoted to the summary of the field notes and recommendations in regard to the elimination of child labour.

Besides the seven chapters, the report also includes a detailed and exhaustive Bibliography on the subject concerned. The question schedule has also been included in the report.

REFERENCES

1. Sukumar, David, Interpretations on Combating Child Labour, IRDS-ILO-IPEC Programme Against Child Labour, India, 1996, p. 6.
2. The right to be a child, UNICEF House, New Delhi, 1994, p. 5.
3. Maria, De La Luz Silva, "Urban Poverty and Child Work, Elements for the Analysis of Child Work in Chile", in Garry Rodgers and Guy Standing (eds.), Child Work, Poverty and Under-development, ILO, Geneva, 1981, p. 160.
4. Ivy, George, Child Labour and Child Work, Ashish Publishing House, New Delhi, 1990, p. 17.
5. Census of India, Provisional Population Total Workers and Non Workers, Paper 3 Series, India, 1981, p. 2
6. Moddie, A.D., The Concept of Work in Indian Society, Indian Institute of Advanced Study, Shimla, and Manohar Publications, New Delhi, 1990, p. xiii.
7. Ivy, George, op. cit, p. 18
8. National Institute of Human Resource Development, Labour Welfare—A tool for Industrial Peace and Productivity, Monograph, Chennai, 1990, p. 1
9. Ibid.
10. Ivy, George, op. cit, p. 17.
11. Sukumar, David, op. cit, p. 8
12. Pati, R.N., Rehabilitation of Child Labourers in India, Ashish Publishing House, New Delhi, 1989, p. 44.
13. Report of the Director General of the International Labour Organisation, 1983.
14. Devi, Laxmi, Encyclopaedia of Child and Family Welfare, Vol. 4, Institute for Sustainable Development Lucknow and Anmol Publications Pvt. Ltd., New Delhi, 1998, p. 2.
15. Fyfe, Alec, Child Labour: A Guide to Project Design, International Labour Office, Geneva, 1993.

16. Quoted in Kulshrestha, Jinesh Chandra, Child Labour in India, Ashish Publishing House, New Delhi, 1978, pp. 1-2.
17. Tripathy, S.N., Child Labour in India — Issues and Policy Options, Discovery Publishing House, New Delhi, 1996, p. 119.
18. Devi, Laxmi, op. cit., p. 302.
19. Award Digest, Journal of Labour Legislation, Vol. XX, No. 7-12.
20. Pinto, G.J., Paper presented on UNICEF Programme — Approaches Advocated to Respond to Street Children in India, 1996.
21. Rane, Asha, Street Children — A Challenge to the Social Work Profession, Tata Institute of Social Sciences, Published by Sheilu Sreenivasan, Bombay, 1994, p. 182.
22. Vinay, D. Lall, Informal Sector in the National Capital Region, B.R. Publishing Corporation, Delhi, 1989, p. 5.
23. Kudamala, Sreeramamurty, Urban Labour in Informal Sector, B.R. Publishing Corporation, Delhi, 1986.
24. Keith, Hart, "Informal Income Opportunities and Urban Employment in Ghana", in Journal of Modern African Studies, London, February 1973, p. 61-89.
25. Mathew, P.M., Informal Sector in India: Critical Perspectives, Khama Publishers, New Delhi, 1995, p. 36.
26. The Urban Informal Sector in Developing Countries, ILO, Geneva, 1981, p. 17.
27. Ivy, George, op. cit., p. 32.
28. Bjorkman, James Warner, The Changing Divisions of Labour in South Africa, Manohar Publications, 1987.
29. Devi, Laxmi, op. cit., p. 220.
30. Ibid., p. 221.
31. Mendelievich, Children at Work, International Labour Office, Geneva, 1979.
32. Annual Report of Asha Nivas Social Service Centre, Chennai, 1996-97, p. 2.
33. Report on National Seminar on Implementation of Child Labour Projects, National Resource Centre on Child Labour, V.V. Giri National Labour Institute, Noida, 1997, p. 2.
34. Kulshreshtra, J.C., op. cit.
35. Mustafa, Mohd. and Sharma, Onkar, Child Labour in India - A Bitter Truth, Deep and Deep Publications, New Delhi, 1996.
36. Burra, Neera, Born to Work, Child Labour in India, Oxford University Press, New Delhi, 1995.
37. Sharma, B.K. and Mittar, Vishwa, Child Labour and Urban Informal Sector, Deep and Deep Publications, New Delhi, 1990.
38. Bhargava, Pramila H., The Elimination of Child Labour Whose Responsibility?, Sage Publications, New Delhi, 2003.
39. Mishra, Lakshmidhar, Child Labour in India, Oxford University Press, New Delhi, 2000.

40. Mendelievich, Children at Work, International Labour Office, Geneva, 1979.
41. Singh, A.N., The Child Rag-Pickers Socio-Economic Perspectives and Intervention Strategies, Shipra Publications, Delhi, 1996.
42. Singh, A.N., Child Labour in India Socio-Economic Perspectives, Shipra Publications, Delhi, 1990.
43. Anker, Richard, Barge, Sandhya, Rajagopal, S. and Joseph, M.P. (eds.), Economics of Child Labour in Hazardous Industries of India, Centre for Operations Research and Training, Baroda, 1998.
44. Tripathy, S.K., Child Labour in India, Discovery Publishing House, New Delhi, 1989.
45. Weiner, Myron, The Child and the State in India, Oxford University Press, Delhi, 1991.
46. Shukla, B.N. and Shukla, Bimla, "Child Labour in the Informal Sector", Paper presented at Annual Conference of the Indian Society of Labour Economics (ISLE), Bhubaneswar, 1990.
47. Patil, B.R., Working Children in Urban India, D.B. Publishers (P) Ltd., Bangalore, 1988.
48. Singh, I.S., Child Labour, Oxford & IBH Publishing Co. Pvt. Ltd., New Delhi, 1992.
49. Tripathy, S.N., Exploitation of Child Labour in Tribal India, Daya Publishing House, Delhi, 1991.
50. Mohsin, Nadeen, "Poverty, Breeding Ground of Child Labour", in Mainstream, Vol. 18, No. 41, 1980, pp. 27-29.
51. Verma, V., "Child Labour Need for Social Awareness", in Yojana, Vol. 23, No. 2, 1979, pp. 13-14.
52. Murthy, G.K. and Rani, T.J., "Wages of Child Labour", in Yojana, Vol. 27, No. 18, 1983, pp. 12-14.

2

Child Labour in India

Today, child labour is almost non-existent in the industrialized countries where it was prevalent during earlier times. However, the predominance of child labour in many developing countries continues to be quite pronounced, although reliable data are scanty. By and large, the greater the importance of agriculture and related activities, the greater is the use of child labour.[1]

Child labour is a colossal problem in India. Data reveals that India has the largest number of child labourers in the world. The ILO estimates that the number of working children in the 5-14 age group in the developing countries in 250 million, of whom at least 120 million are working full time. Of these 61 per cent are in Asia, 32 per cent in Africa, and 7 per cent are in Latin America. According to 1991 census, the total child population of India in the 0-14 age group is 297 million out of a total population of 846 million.[2] Of this 11.28 million are reported to be working children. Of this (297 million) 203 million are in the age group of 5-14, the school-going age. Out of 203 million children, 112 million are reported to have been enrolled in the formal school system, about 7 million are in the non-formal education and about 100 million are nowhere children which means they are out of school.[3] If we take into account the number of working children in the States, Andhra Pradesh tops the list with 1,661,940 million.

The state-wise distribution of child labour in 11 major states, according to 1971, 1981 and 1991 census, is presented in Table 2.1.[4]

Thus, we see that there has been a decline in the overall population of working children during 1981-91. The number of working children, according to the 1971 census was 10.75 million, which increased to 13.64 million (1981 census), representing an increase of 26.88 per cent. As per the 1991 census, the working children population decreased to 11.28 million, which means that the number has fallen by 17.3 per cent during 1981-91.

Table 2.1: Child Labour in Eleven Major States

	States	*1971*	*1981*	*1991*
1.	Andhra Pradesh	1,627,492	1,951,312	1,661,940
2.	Uttar Pradesh	1,326,726	1,434,675	1,410,086
3.	Madhya Pradesh	1,112,319	1,698,597	1,352,563
4.	Maharashtra	988,357	1,557,756	1,068,418
5.	Karnataka	808,719	1,131,530	976,247
6.	Bihar	1,059,359	1,101,764	942,245
7.	Rajasthan	587,389	819,605	774,199
8.	West Bengal	511,443	605,263	711,691
9.	Tamil Nadu	713,305	975,055	578,889
10.	Gujarat	518,061	616,913	523,585
11.	Orissa	492,477	702,293	452,394
	Total (All India)	**10,753,985**	**13,640,870**	**11,285,349**

Origin of Child Labour

So far as the origin of child labour is concerned, it has its roots in two traditions — (i) from children learning their disciplines and skills of work from their parents; and (ii) from bonded labour where a young child is given to a landlord in lieu of debt repayment and the landlord uses him or her as his bonded servant. Vagrant and illegal trades also attract a few youngsters as easy money through low wages make their life temporarily comfortable. Besides this, urbanization, rapid industrialization and growing unemployment amongst adults, too have a contributory effect on the employment of children.[5]

If we go back to Kautilya's Arthashastra, we find that there is a mention of employment of children in India in the form of slavery. During this period (3rd century B.C.) child slaves, who were less than eight years of age, were known to be working in many nobles houses. During the medieval period, there were certain crafts which totally depended on the employment of children. As such, children were normally placed as trainees under artisans and craftsman. Even now this tradition continues especially in carpet, cotton and silk weaving industries. These industries employ a large number of children to perform various activities related to these industries.

The phenomenon of child labour was prevalent all over the world, in the pre-industrial revolution phase, though it had an altogether different nature and magnitude. During the post industrial revolution phase, child labour became a growing phenomenon upto the first half of this century in industrialized countries. In case of developing countries, it still continues to grow. With the economic recession, this problem was expected to become more acute. It has started making its appearance in industrialized countries. It is also witnessed in the third world, in general and in India in particular, as a result of persistent poverty and the population explosion.

However, now the nature and magnitude of the problem of child labour is largely different. But in case of India, some of the past characteristics of this problem are still present. Although, all over the world, children are exploited through wage employment and self-employment, still almost nowhere else does this problem feature so high in the priority of government and non-governmental organization.[6]

Rapid urbanization has made the problem of child labour more visible because of its association with work outside the family context and high rate of rural-urban migration of both the family and individual types. In case of a developing country like India, we find that the children mainly work in small manufacturing units as cheap labour. We also find that due to technical innovations in the urban sector, children are often forced into street trades turning child labour into casual labour.[7]

Thus we see that child labour has existed in one form or the other in all historical times. However, a significant change that has taken place, is its hazardous nature and graver magnitude that has made its perception as a social problem.

Constitutional Provisions

Since beginning India has followed a pro-active policy with regard to handling the problem of child labour. This is clearly visible in the Constitution of India, especially, Part III and IV i.e., the Chapter on Fundamental Rights and Directive Principles of State Policy. A number of legislations exist which specifically prohibit employment of children below the prescribed age such as Factories Act, Mines Act, Merchant Shipping Act, Shops and Commercial Establishing Act, Beedi and Cigar Workers Act, etc.

Some of the constitutional provisions are mentioned below:

Article 23: Prohibition of traffic in human beings and forced labour.

Traffic in human beings and beggar and other similar forms of forced labour are prohibited and any contravention of this provision shall be an offence punishable in accordance with law.

Article 24: Prohibition of employment of children in factories etc.

No child below the age of fourteen years shall be employed to work in any factory or mine or engaged in any other hazardous employment.

Article 39 (e) and (f): certain principles of policy to be followed by state.

The state shall, in particular, direct its policy securing (e) that the health and strength of workers, men and women and the tender age of children are not abused and that citizens are not forced by economic necessity to enter avocations unsuited to their age or strength, (f) that children are given opportunities and facilities to develop in a healthy manner and in conditions of freedom and dignity and that childhood and youth are protected against exploitation and against moral and material abandonment.

Article 41: The right to work, to education and to public assistance in particular circumstances:

The state shall within the limits of its economic capacity and development make effective provision for securing the right to work, to education and to public assistance in cases of unemployment, old age, sickness, and disablement and in other cases of undeserved want.

Article 45: Provision for free and compulsory education for children.

The state shall endeavour to provide within a period of 10 years from the commencement of this Constitution for free and compulsory education for all children until they complete the age of fourteen years.

Article 47: Responsibility of the state to raise the nutritional levels, and standards of living of its citizens and to improve public health.

The State shall regard the raising of the level of nutrition and the standard of living of its people and improvement of public health as among its primary duties and in particular the state shall endeavour to bring about prohibition of the consumption except for medical purposes of intoxicating drinks and of drugs, which are injurious to health.

Legal Protection of Children at Work

With regard to legal protection of children at work, the policy of the Government had been to ban employment of children below the age of 14 years in factories, mines and hazardous employments and to regulate the working conditions of children in other employments. To achieve this basic objective, the Child Labour (Prohibition and Regulation) Act was enacted in 1986. The working conditions of children have been regulated in all employments which are not prohibited under the Child Labour (Prohibition and Regulation) Act, through a Notification dated 26.5.93. Following up on a preliminary Notification issued on 26.5.93, Government have also prohibited employment of children in the following occupation and processes — adding to the six occupations and fourteen processes already scheduled under the Act for such prohibition:

i) Abattoirs/slaughter houses,
ii) "Hazardous processes", as defined in Section (2cb) and "dangerous operations" as notified under Rules made with reference to Section 87 of the Factories Act, 1948 (63 of 1948),
iii) "Printing" as defined in Section 2 (k) (iv) of the Factories Act (63 of 1948),
iv) Cashew and cashew nut descaling and processing, and
v) Soldering, processes in electronic industries.
vi) Passenger, goods mail transport by Railway,
vii) Carpet weaving,
viii) Cinder picking cleaning of ash pits,
ix) Cement manufacturing,
x) Building operation, construction,
xi) Cloth printing,
xii) Dyeing, weaving,
xiii) Manufacturing of matches, explosives, fireworks,
xiv) Catering, establishment in Railway premises or port limits,
xv) Beedi making,

xvi) Mica cutting, splitting,
xvii) Wool cleaning,

In occupations and processes electronic other than the above mentioned work by children is permissible only for six hours between 8 a.m. and 7 p.m. with one day's weekly rest. No child shall be permitted or required to work overtime. No child shall be required or permitted to work in any establishment on any day on which he has already been working in another establishment.

The National Policy on Child Labour, 1987

Following the Act, a comprehensive policy, namely, National Child Labour Policy 1987 was adopted. The policy provides a broad framework for tackling various problems of child labour through a number of initiatives. The initiatives are:

i) legislative action plan;
ii) focusing of general development programmes for benefiting children wherever possible; and
iii) project based action plans in areas of high concentration of child labour engaged in various wage employments.

i) *Legislative Action Plan* — The legal action plan seeks to emphasize strict and effective enforcement of the provisions of the Child Labour (Prohibition and Regulation) Act, 1986, the Factories Act, 1948, the Mines Act, 1952, the Plantation Labour Act, 1951, and other Acts containing provisions relating to the employment of children.

ii) *Focussing General Development Programmes to Benefit Child Labour* — A number of national development programmes exist with wide coverage in the areas of education, health, nutrition, integrated child development, and income and employment generation for the poor. It was hoped that with the help of these programmes, a proper environment will be created where the compulsions to send the children to work diminish and children are encouraged to attend school rather than take wage employment.

iii) *Project Based Plan of Action* — The main focus under this was to take up projects in areas of high concentration of working children. The specific sectors of employment where the incidence of child labour is high, are:

i) The match industry in Sivakasi, Tamilnadu.
ii) The diamond polishing industry in Surat, Gujarat.
iii) The precious stone polishing industry in Jaipur, Rajasthan.
iv) The glass industry in Ferozabad, Uttar Pradesh.
v) The brassware industry in Moradabad, Uttar Pradesh.
vi) The handmade carpet industry in Mirzapur — Bhadohi, Uttar Pradesh.
vii) The lock-making industry in Aligarh, Uttar Pradesh.
viii) The handmade carpet industry in Jammu and Kashmir.
ix) The slate industry in Mandsaur, Madhya Pradesh.
x) The slate industry in Markapur in Andhra Pradesh.

The child workers who are involved in these sectors of employment deserve special attention because of the fact that either the employments processes in which they work are prohibited under the Factories Act, or the Child Labour (Prohibition and Regulation) Act or the work is such that it is likely to affect the child's well-being. In each of the 10 "project areas", the thrust should be on following activities:

i) Stepping up the enforcement of the Child Labour (Prohibition and Regulation) Act, the Factories Act and the Mines Act. If necessary, special enforcement staff will be created for the purpose.
ii) Coverage of families of child labour under the income/employment generating programmes under the overall aegis of poverty alleviation programmes.
iii) Where there is a concentration of SC/ST families with child labour, a concentration of special component and Tribal sub-plans by the State Governments in each project area.
iv) Formal and non-formal education of child labour and stepping up programmes of adult education for the parents of working children.
v) Setting up special schools for working children where provision for education, vocational training, supplementary nutrition, health care, etc. would be made. If necessary, stipends would be given to children taken out of banned forms of employment to compensate for their loss in earnings.

vi) Coordinating the activities of different Departments, Ministries of the Central Government and State Governments to benefit child labour.

vii) Creation of awareness through social activist groups and by other means so as to educate people regarding the undesirable aspects of child labour.

National Child Labour Projects (NCLP)

The NCLP's were launched in 1994 in Sambalpur, Thane and Gharma. The main objectives of NCLP were: i) rehabilitation of children withdrawn from work; and ii) prevention of the entry of children to work. It rests on a gradual, sequential, progressive and selective approach to the elimination of child labour. One of the main activity under NCLP is the setting up of Rehabilitation/ NCLP Centres for mainstreaming working children to formal system of education. Welfare inputs provided under NCLP are: non-formal education; vocational/craft training; stipend and nutrition.

Components of NCLP

The NCLP had a number of components. Some of them are as follows:

i) Setting up enforcement of child labour laws.

ii) Imparting non-formal education to enable the children released from work to receive functional literacy and acquire a level of equivalence with the corresponding grade and level in the formal system.

iii) Income and employment generation.

iv) Raising public awareness.

v) Supplementary nutrition through midday meals.

vi) Adult education.

vii) Survey and evaluation.

NCLPs are implemented at the district level through Project Societies formed specially for that purpose. The Chairman of these project societies are usually the collectors of the respective districts. Since all districts have District Rural Development Agencies (DRDA) too, of which also the Collectors are Chairmen, it is only appropriate that linkages be established between the two bodies to ensure that parents of children withdrawn from work and children themselves wherever feasible are covered under various schemes at the district level.

So far as the organizational structure is concerned, it can be found at three levels.

At the national level, the Central Monitoring Committee under the Chairmanship of Secretary (Labour) with representatives from the State Governments reviews the overall functioning of the Child Labour projects.

At the State level, the functioning of the projects are monitored at the state level by the respective State Labour Secretaries or the concerned department.

At the district level, the District Collector periodically reviews the performance of the child labour project under implementation in the district.

The NCLP Centres are being run by NGOs, Voluntary Organisations, Panchayati Raj Institutions, trade unions, youth organizations, mahila mandals/samiti, Yuvak Sangh and project societies, if appropriate NGOs/VOs are not available.

Under the NCLP, the Ministry of Labour, through NGOs, had set up 20 special schools in the carpet producing belts of the eastern part of the Uttar Pradesh in order to provide non-formal education, mid-day meals and a stipend of Rs. 100 per month to the children withdrawn from the carpet trade. A similar project had also been undertaken in the neighbouring state of Bihar for rehabilitation of 500 child labourers withdrawn from the industry.[8]

Initially twelve NCLPs were sanctioned in the eight states (Table 2.1). By 1995-96, seventy-six NCLPs had been sanctioned including the twelve initial projects. These have opened 1,800 special schools under them with about 2,500 teachers, in which about 1.05 lakh children who had been released from hazardous industries/occupations/processes have been enrolled.[9]

National Authority for Elimination of Child Labour

As a follow up of the then Prime Minister, Shri Narasimha Rao's Independence Day speech on August 15, the National Authority for Elimination of Child Labour (NAECL) was set up on 26

September, 1994 to tackle the problem of child labour in a coordinated manner. Shri P.A. Sangma, then Union Labour Minister, was the chairman of NAECL. It comprised of the Secretary, Ministry of Labour and Secretaries of nine other departments and ministries of the Government of India.

Table 2.2: National Child Labour Projects

S. No.	*State*	*Area*	*Employment*	*Coverage of Children*
1.	Uttar Pradesh	Ferozabad	Glass	500
2.		Moradabad	Brassware	500
3.		Aligarh	Locks	500
4.		Mirzapur & Bhadohi	Carpet	2,500
5	Andhra Pradesh	Markapur	Slate	1,000
6.		Jaggampet	Tile	100
7.	Tamil Nadu	Sivakasi	Match & Fireworks	2,350
8.	Madhya Pradesh	Mandsaur	Slate	900
9.	Bihar	Garhwa	Carpet	450
10.	Rajasthan	Jaipur	Gems	1,000
11.	Maharashtra	Thane	Agri-chemicals	2,000
12.	Orissa	Sambalpur	Beedi	3,000

The NAECL was to perform these functions:

i) to lay down the policies and programmes for elimination of child labour particularly in hazardous employments;
ii) to monitor the progress of implementation of programmes, projects and schemes for elimination of child labour, and
iii) to coordinate implementation of child labour elimination related projects of the various sister ministries of the Government of India.

The NAECL resolved to tackle the problem of child labour by a planned, concerted and coordinated effort involving various wings of the Central and State Governments and the NGOs. The purpose of securing convergence of services under the NAECL, was to provide education and health inputs for children taken out of schools in a cost-effective manner, pooling the financial and manpower resources of various ministries. Besides, it was also to provide means of economic sustenance for the parents of children taken out of work. Further, it was sought to create awareness amongst parents such that future flow of children into the world of work is pre-empted.

The NAECL in June 1995, provided guidance and direction to the Ministry of Labour as to how the scheme to eliminate child labour in hazardous occupations, announced by Shri P.V. Narasimha Rao, can be put into operation. Accordingly, the NAECL made some recommendations. These are:

i) To launch a publicity blitz through the electronic and print media to sensitize society against child labour.
ii) To launch the programme to eliminate child labour in hazardous occupations in the 100 most child labour endemic districts of the country by asking them to submit project proposals based on the NCLP scheme to the Ministry of Labour for sanction.

Thus, we see that a number of laws and legislations were made/passed in order to solve the problem of child labour. However, these legislations were only of a transitional nature. Still a lot remains to be done in order to achieve the ultimate goal of child labour welfare.

In order to solve the problem of child labour, it becomes important to identify the causes of child labour in India. Accordingly, in the succeeding pages, the various factors contributing to employment of children in India has been dealt with.

Causes of Child Labour

The reason for employing children are many. A large number of them start working because of being orphaned, rejected by parents or because of broken families and other domestic problems. Sometimes they work in order to supplement family income especially when it is not possible to meet the requirements of the family. Perhaps this is the most important cause of Child Labour in India.

Poverty

Widespread poverty is one the major causes of child labour in India. In a country like India, where around 33 per cent people live below poverty line, where families, are large in size, a general opinion is that any addition to the family income helps to ease the burden of a very tedious existence. As a result, parents are forced to send their children to work. Their income supplements the family income and takes care of illness and other contingencies which demand extra money in hand.

One of the pilot studies conducted in Madras, Madurai and Coimbatore, [10] reveals that about three-fourth of the children were working in order to supplement their family income and about 23 per cent because of the death of their father or guardian.

Another study of working children in Bombay[11] found that low economic status of the family was the most important factor contributing to their non-schooling and their coming into the labour market.

A still another study of working children in Khurja potteries[12] found that those children were working whose parents had less than five bighas of land and these children were contributing to the family income.

Most case studies of child labour do indeed identify the poverty of the household and low level of parental education as important factors in determining the incidence of child labour. [13]

Lack of Parental Interest

This is visible mostly in the rural areas. The rural people are not exposed to education and are unaware of the benefits which literacy or education can bring. Thus, they do not have faith in the educational system and do not care to avail of the educational opportunities for their children. In their opinion, education has no practical use, as such they are bound to send their children for labour.

This fact has been highlighted in the Madras study. The study found that the working children were from low literacy groups of the society. About 44 per cent of the parents of working children were illiterate and another 33 per cent of them belonged to low literacy groups having studied up to fifth standard only. [14] The data clearly shows that most of the parents were not aware of the importance of education. Their only concern was to get monetary benefit out of children's employment.

Migration to Urban Areas

Urbanisation has led to migration of children from their rural homes to the cities in order to find employment. This factor has been dealt with in some of the studies. [15] The Bombay study revealed that 58.2 per cent of the child labour was the exclusive result of the internationalization of the urban slum culture, as their families had migrated to cities before their birth. In all, there were 90 per cent of them who belonged to migrated families.

K.D. Gangrade's study[16] of Delhi found that there is a substantial number of migrants among child workers, particularly in the field of domestic services. Besides domestic work, they were also working in tea-stalls, 'dhabas', hawking evening newspapers, rag-pickers, etc. Most of the child workers had migrated from Almora and Garhwal districts of north-eastern Uttar Pradesh, Azamgarh, Gorakhpur, Gonda, and Basti districts of Uttar Pradesh and, to some extent, from Bihar.

Traditional Attitudes

In a rural set up, the parents teach their children a traditional craft at a very early age so that when they grow up, they become proficient in a job which can become a source of income for them. They believe that if the training is given since childhood, they can learn better because their body is more flexible and pliable and can hence bend, twist, stretch more easily to acquire postures required for particular jobs. Thus, the child becomes a bread winner.

In one of the studies on lock industries of Aligarh[17] it was found that 15.75 per cent of the working children had joined the lock industry because of their family traditions.

Carpet weaving, pottery, silk and cotton weaving, wood carving, carpentary etc. are some of the traditional crafts taught to children within their homes. Craftsmen train their children in their hereditary crafts since early childhood as it is an asset in the learning process. Even musicians and dancers start to train their children at the early age of 5 or 6.[18]

Economic Constraints

Economic constraint is another cause of child labour. Due to this constraint, parents do not feel like sending their children to school to get education, as it costs something. Even if the tuition fee is free, there are other requirements-buying books, uniforms and stationery, to be met. Thus, it means that besides earning for survival, the poor parents have to earn in order to meet the expenses of their children's education. As per the assessment of the PROBE Survey, a minimum of Rs.318 is spent annually towards the education of one child per year.[19] Besides, the Indian Education System is such, that it does not offer job-oriented courses for the children in the rural and urban areas. The existing education system rather prepares the child only for white collared jobs and that too they are offered to those with an undergraduate degree.

Secondly, in India, there is no provision for compulsory education. The provision of compulsory education upto a prescribed age would compel the parents to send their children to schools, leaving hardly any scope for their employment. In a study on Aligarh lock industries it was s found that 41 per cent of the child labour were illiterate, 31 per cent had left the school before passing the fifth standard and only 28 per cent had studied upto middle standard.[20]

Thus we see that a number of factors are responsible for child labour in India. Professor Gangrade is of the opinion that child labour is a result of various factors such as customs, traditional attitude, lack of school or lack of parental interest to send their children to school, urbanization, industrialization, migration, etc.[21] Besides these, there are certain other factors which are responsible for child labour. Absence of father may be one of them. Unemployment, poor standard of living, deep social pruderies, disinterest in study, negative attitude of the parents towards child welfare, irresponsibility of the male members in the family due to drug-addiction, alcoholism, inadequate measures of social security and ineffective law enforcement machinery are some of the other factors contributing to child labour.

Problems of Working Children in India

When we talk about problems of child labour in India, it refers to the various problems which the child faces while working. One of the most important problem is their age. They start working at a very young age. The way they are treated at the work place is really disturbing. They are humiliated and ill-treated and sometimes beaten too.

Secondly, the working hours is not fixed. It varies from 6 to 8 hours per day to even 12 or 14 hours. In a way, the working hours put lots of burden on the shoulders of young children. If we take the case of domestic workers, street hawkers, roadside cafes, those working in dhabas, etc, we find that there is no fixed hours of work.

Third problem is regarding their wage. Here again there is no fixed criteria, as to how the wage has to be given. They are paid much less than an adult worker. The reason given here is that they are inexperienced and the quality and quantity of work produced by them is not the same as compared to the adults. Besides, they have to be trained and it also involves a lot of time and efforts. During the training period, they are not given any payment. If the child gets the job with the help of a labour contractor, he will charge his commission, which is around 25 per cent of child's earning.

Another problem of child labour is the risk involved in some of jobs. If they are working in glass and bangle factory, firework and match-making factory, or are involved in carpet weaving, it means they are exposed to risk. All these occupations are hazardous for children, and can lead to lung problem, accidental burns and other injuries. Some of the chemicals are extremely dangerous and can lead to skin problems and poisoning.

Fourthly, the working condition is not good. The working place is not properly ventilated and sometimes have no light. It is also very unhygienic and usually no first aid facilities are available. Besides, there is no social security and hardly any accident insurance scheme exists.

Fifthly, no health security is provided especially to those who are working on the streets. While working on the streets they brave the weather, whether it is the cold winter evening or the hot summer afternoon, or the rainy season. They are exposed to infectious diseases or develop some deformity. They soon pick up habits like smoking and liquor drinking. Some of them also become drug addicts and spend time in gambling, smuggling or similar criminal activities. They are also exposed to traffic hazards and continue to work even if they are ill.

Thus, we see that the working children face a lot of problem at their work place. The energy which should have been spent on nurturing talent, capacity and power is used for the purpose of bare survival. It arrests or distorts the natural growth process of a child to full adulthood. It deprives them of educational opportunities, minimizes their chance for vocational training and forces them to remain unskilled labourers with low wages. As a result of all these, "he spends his whole life at the bottom of the social ladder, performing routine, unskilled jobs, when he is not out of job altogether."[22]

Summing Up

Since long, efforts have been made consistently to improve the conditions of working children. Various policies and schemes have been formulated from time to time both at the national and international level. The International Labour Organisation (ILO) since its inception has paid special attention to child labour. The member countries have also adopted and enforced its recommendations by enacting and enforcing statutory enactments on the subject of child labour. In this direction, a number of Acts have been passed in India. However, unfortunately, desired results could not be achieved so far. A number of reasons can be attributed to it, for example, defective drafting of statutory enactments and the gap involved there in, lack of effective implementation process, indifferent attitude of the general masses, etc. As a result, it has been realized that it is an uphill task having multifarious dimensions and the problem involves many complexities and intricacies which can be tackled in a planned and systematic manner. We cannot succeed unless social awakening is created among the common masses and public opinion is built up against the employer exploiting child labour.

The International Labour Organisation, in its report[23] of 1980, holds that child labour in general should be gradually eliminated because of:

a) the physical and mental havoc wrought by it;
b) the displacement of adult workers in effect by child workers; and
c) the lowering of adult earning power due to its prevalence.

After going through the magnitude of the problem of child labour, the causes of child labour and the problems they face while working, one feels that there is a need to launch a determined attack in order to solve the problem of child labour in India. Some of the remedial measures to solve the problems of child labour are as follows:

i) wherever employment of children is permitted, the legislative measures aiming at the welfare of the child labour should be fully implemented;
ii) wherever possible, the NGOs and voluntary organizations should be involved in solving the problem. The NGOs and voluntary organizations, with the financial support of the Government, should impart non-formal education, health care, nutrition and vocational training to the child labourers and family counseling to the parents; and
iii) the NGOs should make efforts to involve the local public and parents/guardians of child labourers and train them on child development. Besides, they should be made aware of the efforts taken by the government and NGO's for upliftment of child labour.

REFERENCES

1. International Labour Office, "Employment Prospects of Children and Young People in Asia," in International Labour Review, Vol. 88, 1963.
2. Mishra, Lakshmidhar, Child Labour in India, Oxford University Press, New Delhi, 2000, p. 35.
3. Ibid.
4. ILO — IIPA Action Programme No. 090.92.325.254 on Elimination of Child Labour, Indian Institute of Public Administration, New Delhi, 1999, p. 1.
5. Child Labour Series, Working Children in India, Child Labour Cell, Noida, December 1993.
6. Jain, Mahaveer, Child Labour in India, A Select Bibliography, National Labour Institute, Noida, 1994.
7. Ibid., p. 5.
8. Speech of Shri G. Venkat Swamy, Former Union Minister of Textiles, Delivered at the Workshop of District Collectors/District Heads on "Towards Eliminating Child Labour", held at Vigyan Bhawan, September 13-14, 1995.
9. Mishra, Lakshmidhar, op. cit., p. 200.

10. George, K.N., "Child Labour in the City of Madras", Paper presented to a National Seminar on Employment of Children in India, organized by National Institute of Public Cooperation and Child Development, New Delhi, August, 1977 (Unpublished).
11. Study of Child Labour in Bombay, National Institute of Public Cooperation and Child Development, New Delhi, 1978, (Unpublished).
12. Burra, Neera, "Where Children are Last in Misery's Mould", in The Hindustan Times, February 14, 1988, p. 5.
13. ILO, World Development Report, ILO, Geneva, 1992.
14. George, K.N., op. cit.
15. Study of Child Labour in Bombay, op. cit.
16. Gangrade, K.D., Child Labour in India, Department of Social Work, University of Delhi, Delhi, 1978-79 (Unpublished).
17. Kulshreshtha, Jinesh Chandra, Indian Child Labour, Uppal Publishing House, New Delhi, 1994, p. 42.
18. Mustafa, Mohd. and Sharma, Onkar, Child Labour in India — A Bitter Truth, Deep and Deep Publications, New Delhi, 1996, p. 7.
19. Bhargava, Pramila H., The Elimination of Child Labour: Whose Responsibility? Sage Publications, New Delhi, 2003, p. 61.
20. Kulshreshtha, Jinesh Chandra, op. cit., p. 39.
21. Gangrade, K.D., op. cit.
22. Mustafa, Mohd. and Sharma, Onkar, op. cit., p. 6.
23. Kulshreshtha, Jinesh Chandra, op. cit., p. 21.

3

ILO's and UNICEF's Concern for the Child

Since the proclamation in 1979 as the "International year of the Child" by the United Nations General Assembly, the call for action and study was taken up by many people and organizations all over the world. Some organizations studied child nutrition, others child education and still others child welfare in general. The International Labour Organisation made its special contribution by studying child labour. Presently working as a specialized agency of the United Nations Organisation, the ILO is widely viewed as the international agency concerned with child labour. It was created after the First World War, in 1919, as part of the League of Nations. India was one among the first ten founding, non-elective, and permanent members of the ILO and has, therefore, a special mandate, and special place in this international body.[1]

Since the very beginning, the ILO has devoted an important part of its standard-setting activity to the abolition of child labour. Several months after its foundation in 1919, the ILO adopted a convention prohibiting work by children under 14 years of age in industrial undertakings. Other conventions followed, outlawing child work at sea, in fishing, agriculture, non-industrial enterprises and mines.[2] It has enacted as many as nineteen conventions to prohibit child labour in different sectors and under different conditions.

Despite these conventions and national and international standards, we find that a number of children are engaged in those activities which are in violation of these conventions and standards. These activities include,[3] for example:

i) young girls working in small industrial enterprises in

tasks that involve handling microscopically fine wires, finally resulting in loss of eye sight within five to eight years;

ii) shepherd boys subcontracted to owners of large estates to work for as long as 15 hours a day;

iii) children employed as seasonal and cheap labour in pesticide — soaked fields;

iv) children working underground in mines;

v) children working as bonded labourers;

vi) children employed in street trades practically found everywhere in the third world countries;

vii) children engaged in numerous small industrial workshops and service establishments.

The ILO clearly differentiates between child labour and child work. According to ILO, child work is that work where children are truly a part of the socialization process and a means of transmitting skills from parents to child. Whereas child labour is that situation where children are compelled to work in a regular or continuous basis to earn a living for themselves or their families.[4]

Out of these two, i.e., child work and child labour, the ILO is concerned with the latter. The ILO has followed a dual policy vis-à-vis child labour. The first policy is the effective abolition of child labour. It can be achieved when the countries carry out a series of legal and socio-economic measures, such as, improving the living standards, fuller or higher levels of adult employment. Since the adoption and successful implementation of such measures will take time, hence the ILO puts forth the second policy, i.e., the protection of children at work. To achieve this objective, the ILO suggests that the countries should regulate the conditions in which children work, for example, shorter hours of work, improved wages and remuneration, safer and less hazardous working conditions, etc.

Thus, we see that, in the long run, if we want to eliminate child labour, it requires a general improvement of living standards, a reinforcement of the educational infrastructure and, perhaps most importantly, a greater consciousness of the need for change. On the other hand, in the long run, the protection of working children requires practical measures that can improve their working and living conditions.[5]

So far as the causes of child labour is concerned, we find that the problem has its genesis in socio-economic environment in which the masses live. The ILO has listed major causes of child labour in developing countries.[6] Their contribution to the phenomenon of child labour is shown against each:

Sl. No.	*Causes*	*Intensity*
1.	Poverty	23.4%
2.	Need to assist parents in household economic activity	32.9%
3.	Parents want them to work	26.3%
4.	Need to earn their own living	7.9%
5.	Better than doing nothing	6.9%
6.	Other reasons	2.6%

The basic objective of the ILO is the betterment of labour by ensuring international cooperation for some minimum and uniform standards. The ultimate aim of abolition of child labour is not only consistent with its basic objectives and policies, it is an integral part of it.[7] This view has been highlighted/reflected in one of the reports of the International Labour Conference. The report reads:[8] "The abolition of child labour, one of the aims for which the ILO was created, and the promotion of the well-being of children in the fields within the ILO's competence have been the focal points of much of the Organisation's work throughout its existence.

Since inception, attempts have been made by the ILO to regulate child labour in the short term without losing sight of the long-term goal of elimination. The ILO has been endeavouring for adoption and promulgation of measures by its member countries for providing the children, whether already in employment or seeking employment, with protection against exploitation, coercion, maltreatment and bondage. Its regulating and protective work has been expressed in term of international standard setting or conventions. These conventions, are only binding on those member states who ratify them. Once the conventions are ratified by the member states, article 22 of the ILO's Constitution requires signatories to provide annual reports on their compliance, while aricles 24 and 26 allow for the consideration of complaints against a state for failure to live up to the instrument in question.[9]

The ILO adopted its first convention on child labour in the

very year of its inception i.e., 1919. The Minimum Age (Industry) Convention 1919 (No. 5) sets the minimum age for regular industrial work, excluding family enterprise and technical schools, at 14. In 1937, this convention was revised and the minimum age was raised to 15.

During 1920 to 1965, the minimum age conventions were adopted for certain areas (Table 3.1).[10]

Table 3.1: ILO Minimum Age Conventions, 1920-65

Sl. No.	*Occupation*	*Convention*	*Minimum Age*
1.	Seamen	No. 7 1920	14
		No. 58 1936	15
2.	Agriculture	No. 10 1921	14 (except out of school hours).
3.	Mining	No. 123 1965	16
4.	Non-industrial	No. 33 1932	14 (but allows children over 12 to be employed outside of school hours on light work).

A detailed analysis of the ILO conventions on the employment of child labour and young persons, the aims and objectives of these international standards, whether the conventions have been ratified by India and the reasons for their non-ratification is given in Table 3.2.[11]

Table 3.2: ILO Conventions

Sl. No.	*Title of the Convention*	*Aim*	*Status of ratification*
I.	Convention no. 5: Minimum age (Industry) 1919	To prohibit employment of children under the age of 14 in any public or private industrial undertaking	Ratified on 9.9.55.
II.	Convention no. 10:Minimum age (Agriculture) 1921	To provide that children under the age of 14 may not be employed or work in any public or private organizational undertaking or any branch thereof save outside the hours fixed for school attendance	Not ratified, because of lack of resources which will be required for its implementation, as it is related to a vast and unorganized field.

(*Contd...*)

Sl. No.	Title of the Convention	Aim	Status of ratification
III.	Convention no. 33: Minimum age (Non-industrial employment) 1932	To provide that children under 14 or those over 14 years who are still required by national laws or regulations to attend primary school shall not be employed in any employment to which this Convention applies.	Not ratified, because a latter convention on the subject has come into force.
IV.	Convention no. 59: Minimum age (Industry) (Revised) 1937	To prohibit employment of children under the age of 15 in any public or private industrial undertaking.	Not ratified, because of variations in the nature of wide spread mines and lack of effective system of medical examination.
V.	Convention no. 60:Minimum age (Non-industrial employment) (Revised) 1937	To provide that children under 15 years or children over 15 years who are still required by national laws or regulations to attend primary school shall not be employed in any employment to which this Convention applies.	Not ratified, because the subject matter is primarily of the state's concern whose laws on shapes and commercial establishments vary with one another, and, therefore, a national consensus on the issues involved is called for.
VI	Convention no. 123:Minimum age (Underground work) 1965	To provide that persons under 16 years of age shall not be employed or work underground in mines.	Ratified on 20.3.75.
VII	Convention no. 138: Minimum age 1973	The convention relates to the abolition of child labour. The minimum age for admission to employment or work shall be not less than the age of completion of compulsory	Not ratified, because there is absence of an omnibus provision fixing a minimum age of entry to employment.

(Contd...)

Sl. No.	*Title of the Convention*	*Aim*	*Status of ratification*
		schooling (normally not less than 15 years). Developing countries may, however, initially specify a minimum age of 14 years.	
I.	Night Work convention no. 6: Night work for young persons (Industry) 1919	Abolition of night work for young persons in any public or private industrial undertaking. The provisions of the Convention have been modified for India.	Ratified on 14.7.21.
II.	Convention no. 79: Night work for young persons (Non industrial occupation) 1966	To provide that children under 14 years of age who are admissible for full time or part time employment and those over 14 who are still subject to full time compulsory school attendance shall not be employed nor work at night during a period of at least 14 consecutive hours including an interval between 8 p.m. and 8 a.m.	Not ratified, because it requires review at the national level of various state enactments relating to shops and commercial establishments.
III	Convention no. 124: Medical examination of young persons (Underground work) 1965. Seafarer's conditions for admission for employment.	To provide that a thorough medical examination and periodic reexamination at intervals of not more than one year for fitness for employment shall be required for the employment or work in underground mines of persons under 21 years of age.	Not ratified, because of its wide coverage.
I	Convention no. 15: Minimum age (Trimmers, stokers) Convention 1921.	To prohibit employment of young persons of below 18 years as trimmers and stokers in port. If persons of over 18 years are not available then young persons between 16 and 18 can be employed.	Ratified on 20.11.22

(*Contd...*)

Sl. No.	Title of the Convention	Aim	Status of ratification
		Trimmers/stokers below 16 years can be employed, subject to medical fitness, in the coastal trade of India.	
II	Convention no. 16: Medical examination of young persons (Sea) Convention 1921.	Young persons under 18 years of age can be employed on any vessel on the production of a medical certificate attesting fitness for such work.	Ratified on 20.11.22.

Convention No. 138, coupled with Recommendation No. 146, is the most comprehensive international instrument and statement on child labour. Convention No. 138 applies to all areas of economic activity (factories, mines, plantations, the sea, etc.) regardless of whether the children are employed for wages or not.

Convention No. 138 has three Articles, which reads as follows:

Article I: Each member for which this convention is in force undertakes to pursue a national policy designated to ensure the effective abolition of child labour and to raise progressively the minimum age for admission to employment or work to a level consistent with the fullest physical and mental development of young persons.

Article 2: The minimum age specified in pursuance of paragraph 1 of this Article shall not be less than the age of completion of compulsory schooling and, in any case, shall not be less than 15 years.

Article 3: The minimum age for admission to any type of employment or work which by its nature or the circumstances in which it is carried out is likely to jeopardize the health, safety or morals of young persons shall not be less than 18. The main drawback of Convention No. 138 is that it does not speak about a single minimum age, rather it speaks of various minimum ages depending on the type of employment and work (Table 3.3)[12]

Table 3.3: Minimum Age of Entry to Employment in Accordance with Convention No. 138

S. No.	*General minimum age*	*Light work*	*Hazardous Work*
1.	In normal circumstances, 15 years or more (not less than compulsory school age)	13 Years	18 Years (16 years conditionally)
2.	Where economy and educational facilities are insufficiently developed	12 years	18 years (16 years conditionaly)

The Convention No. 138 contains flexible provisions and saving clauses. The figures present a very disappointing picture with regard to its ratification. By 1979 only 13 countries had ratified it and by 1988 this figure rose to 36.[13]

Besides these conventions and recommendations, the ILO has adopted a number of resolutions relating to protection of children and young persons. One of them is the one of 1945 by which the ILO has endeavoured to draw the attention towards the need of maintenance, health, education, employment, protection and general welfare of children and young persons.[14]

ILO Activities to Combat Child Labour

There have been three distinct stages in the activities the organization has undertaken to combat child labour. The first phase was the legislative phase (1919 to 1973). During this phase the ILO was completing their standards upto Convention 138 and Recommendation 146, with the present doctrine in this area. During the second phase, the ILO, through their publications and meetings, exposed the problem publicly by denouncing abuses committed and highlighting the results of certain positive actions. In their third phase, i.e., more recently, the ILO have been involved in a technical assistance phase to help member states who ask for it.

One of the principal ways in which the ILO has tried to combat child labour is through the adoption and application of international labour standards and secondly through International Progamme on the Elimination of Child Labour (IPEC). With the launching of this programme, which is operational since 1992, the

ILO has embarked on a course of action to put an end to this problem.

International Programme on the Elimination of Child Labour (IPEC)

During early 1990s, due to a sudden spurt in global interest on child labour, the ILO launched the IPEC in 1992, with an aim to progressively eliminate child labour worldwide. Initially it was funded by Germany and is now being financed also by Australia, Belgium, Canada, Denmark, the European Commission, France, Italy, Norway, Spain, the United States of America, the United Kingdom, the Netherlands, Luxembourg and Germany. India was the first country to join the programme in May 1992. The IPEC became fully operational in late 1992 when India, Brazil, Kenya, Thailand, Turkey and Indonesia signed it. In 1994, Pakistan, Bangladesh, Nepal, United Republic of Tanzania and Philippines followed suit. By 1996-97 Argentina, Bolivia, Peru, Panama, Egypt, Venezuela, Sri Lanka, Chile, Costa Rica, Cambodia, Equator, Guatemala, Honduras, Nicaragua, Dominican Republic, and El Salvador, were added to the list of participating countries. Today, it is operational in 30 countries.

The IPEC gives priority to the eradication of the most abusive and exploitative types of child labour. It has rightly been described as the ILO's "operational arm" in the fight against child labour. The IPEC is flexible in responding to the country's needs in addressing their specific child labour situation.[15] Its strategy rests on the commitment of individual governments to address child labour in cooperation with employers and workers organizations, non-governmental organizations and the media, in a broad social alliance. A government's will and commitment to do so, are expressed in its signing of a memorandum of understanding with the ILO.[16]

Aim[17] and Objective[18] of IPEC

The main aim of IPEC is the elimination of child labour in a phased manner. It can be done in two ways. Firstly, by strengthening the capability of countries to deal with the problem and secondly, by promoting a worldwide movement to combat child labour. Eventually, this problem can be solved only from within the countries themselves. Thus, ILO-IPEC strives to do certain things. Some of them are:

i) To support national efforts in order to combat child labour and to build up a permanent capacity to tackle the problem.
ii) To give priority to the eradication of the most hazardous and exploitative types of child labour.

To insist on preventive measures.

The ILO — IPEC's has established three priority target groups in order to achieve the ultimate goal of eliminating child labour, which is already in progress. The three priority target groups, are:

Those children who are working under forced labour conditions and are in bondage.

Those children who are in hazardous working conditions and occupations.

Those who are very young working children (under 12 years of age).

Besides these target groups, special attention is also given to working girls, especially those who are vulnerable to exploitation and abuse.

The objectives of this programme were:

i) to contribute substantially in the long term to the elimination of child labour in a selected group of countries;
ii) to enhance the capability of the member states so that they can design and implement policies and programmes to effectively protect working children and combat child labour;
iii) to increase awareness of member states and the international community as a whole as to the dimensions and consequences of child labour and national obligations under international law.

Keeping these objectives in mind, the activities were set, accordingly, in the wider context and the activities were linked to the transitional process of regulation and protection of working children. This came down to a two-track approach: firstly, to provide support where the political will to act existed and secondly, to help mobilize and exert pressure within countries where this was not the case. It was recognized that there was a compelling need to promote a broad social movement that could support, and if need be, stimulate government policy and action. It was expected that NGOs would play a leading role in national campaigns alongside employer's and workers organizations.

So far as India is concerned, the IPEC programme is guided by a National Steering Committee, the Chairman of which is the Secretary, Ministry of Labour. Under IPEC, India has undertaken certain important initiatives, some of which are as follows:[19]

i) Rehabilitation of about one lakh working children employed in hazardous and other extremely adverse conditions across the country;
ii) Sensitizing trade unions in the country to the evils of child labour and motivating them to play a prominent role against it;
iii) Making government and non-government agencies, semi-government institutions, autonomous bodies, etc. aware how important an area of concern it is and building up their capacity to tackle the problem;
iv) Strengthening the managerial capability of project directors of the government NCLPs by developing training modules for them and providing them with training.
v) Conducting research studies to understand the implications of child labour and documenting them;
vi) Training labour inspectors on the effective enforcement of child labour laws, training NGOs and institutions on various aspects relating to child labour, including the design, management, and evaluation of projects for its elimination;
vii) Mobilizing employers and their organizations against child labour and sensitizing them against employment of children;
viii) Setting up a Child Labour Cell in the National Institute of Rural Development (NIRD), Hyderabad, to assist the central and state governments in introducing policy changes to combat child labour in rural areas, training elected personnel and officers of related departments, and developing the capability of the NIRD to conduct action research and undertake the evaluation of child labour projects;
ix) Integration of a child labour component in joint

Government of India-UN products on primary education;

x) Developing training packages to promote sustainable income generation activities for mothers of children rehabilitated from (particularly, intolerable and exploitative) work to substitute the fall in family incomes on account of withdrawal of the child from work; etc.

The Working of IPEC Programme[20]

So far as the working of IPEC programme is concerned, it pursues a phased, multi-sectoral strategy, beginning with a "situational analysis" of the nature and magnitude of child labour in a given country. Assistance in policy design, institution building, awareness raising, development and application of protective legislation and support to direct action are some of the subsequent steps involved in the working of the IPEC.

Thus, we see that the IPEC strives to support, rather than supplant national efforts to combat child labour. The best way to strengthen the capacity of partner organizations, as per ILO-IPEC's thinking, is to apply a phased and multi-sectoral strategy, against child labour so as to establish an international climate conducive to action. This would include the following: the collection and dissemination of statistical information, the networking of government agencies, social partners and NGOs, advocacy through mass media and targeted at policy makers, improved coordination with international agencies, and an international exchange of views and experiences.[21]

With regard to the implementational aspect, it can be said that the IPEC was implemented in a highly decentralized manner. As part of the framework set out in the Memorandum of Understanding with the Government of participating countries, the execution of Action Programmes was subcontracted mainly to NGOs. The National Steering Committees were to look into the development of national programmes. The day to day assistance to the implementation of the national programme and the preparation of information for the National Steering Committee was done by the national programme coordinator. He was supervised by the Director of the ILO Area office and worked under the technical guidance of IPEC at headquarters.

Another body known as the Programme Steering Committee (PSC) was created to review the general strategy of IPEC and of national programmes. The committee also examines a work plan and budget for a period of two-years. The PSC receives annual reports submitted by the office and suggest priorities for the programme. The PSC consists of — one representative of the ILO and the donors, one participating countries representative, one employer and worker representative and observers from UNICEF and UNESCO.

With the help of the IPEC, the ILO got operational capability for the first time. A time-frame of around ten years was set by the ILO-IPEC in order to provide assistance to a given country. This time period is, of course, flexible. Depending on the stage of development, the nature and extent of child labour in the country and the political and public resolve to combat it, some countries may need more time and some may need less.[22]

Under the IPEC, a wide variety of interventions was devised. But rehabilitation of child labour through non-formal education was given a central place. Accordingly, around one lakh working children were rehabilitated under various non-formal education programmes, largely implemented by NGOs. An evaluation of the IPEC conducted in 1999 noted the following:[23]

In most of the schools the children were found happy and eager to learn. This is reflected in a significantly higher (96-98 per cent) level of attendance as well as retention in these schools. The implementation of these programmes has also demonstrated that the beneficiaries and their families were willing to accept adjustments to the consequential income losses.

The evaluation team further found that the IPEC had a significant impact on child labour in the country through a variety of interventions. Both IPEC and the national programme on child labour have reinforced each other. As a result, "the issue of child labour has been brought to the national forefront and a more conducive climate has been created to tackle this problem".[24]

So far as the IPEC's partners are concerned, we have seen that the Ministries of Labour are actively involved in the programmes. Besides, other Ministries concerned, such as, the Ministries of Education, Ministries and Departments dealing with youths, the family, the media, health and social welfare and central coordinating units, such as National Planning Commissions and

Prime Minister's Office, also cooperate in the programmes. Over the years, worker's organizations have become active IPEC partners. They play an important role in raising awareness among their members and child workers, in waging media campaigns and in monitoring children's working conditions.

Another major partner in combating child labour is the wide variety of NGOs, who are often a suitable channel for developing concrete activities, which meet the needs of working children, their families and communities. They also tend to succeed in promoting self-organisation and in involving these groups in planning and implementing the action programme. Many other partners like, the media, the judiciary, health institutions, universities and parliamentarians, have joined IPEC in the fight against child labour.[25]

With regard to the priorities of IPEC, it is found that, the most demanding one is to support measures which aim to halt the intolerable. The priority target groups are children who are particularly vulnerable: those children who are working under forced labour conditions and in bondage; those children who are working in hazardous occupations, those children who are very young, i.e., under the age of 12, and the working girls.[26]

A large number of partner organizations have succeeded in withdrawing children from these types of work or, failing that, in improving their working conditions. However, the eradication of these forms of child labour would require huge resources, which is far beyond the resources available to IPEC. Along with this, sheer numbers of children involved and the infrastructure needed to accommodate them, pose a formidable challenge that few partner organizations are equipped to meet.

IPEC has further sharpened its focus on priorities. It has launched a new programme "Action against the most intolerable" forms of child labour (AMIC) during 1997-2001. AMIC specifically supports those programmes which aim at the immediate eradication of bonded child labour; the commercial sexual exploitation of and trafficking in children; child labour in domestic service; child labour in dangerous industries, occupations and working conditions.

There are two categories of IPEC programmes viz. i) action programmes and ii) mini programmes. The action programmes deals with specific issues. Under this programme education (part time or full-time) is provided in non-formal education centres. The main aim of these programmes is to strengthen the capabilities of institutions and partner groups in order to sustain efforts towards the elimination of child labour. Most of these programmes were implemented through NGOs. On the other hand, the main aim of mini programmes is to help partner organizations to carry out preparatory activities (surveys, training or meetings) for possible future action programmes, awareness raising activities and evaluation and audits of IPEC activities.

On the basis of what has been discussed in the preceeding pages, it can be said that the ILO under its IPEC has done a lot in order to combat child labour. But still an enormous amount of work remains to be done in order to eliminate this problem and the phenomenon will continue for many years to come. While the ILO-IPEC initiatives were undoubtedly the most significant international initiatives against child labour in India, there have also been other important ones. The UNICEF is one of them. It has played an important role by supporting government and NGO activities in this area. Accordingly, in the succeeding pages an attempt has been made to analyse the role of UNICEF in combating child labour.

UNICEF and Child Labour

UNICEF is the principal agency for child labour because of its specific responsibility for child labour welfare. UNICEF urges on the need of giving priority to efforts for the immediate elimination of hazardous and exploitative child labour and urgent support for education, so that children may acquire the knowledge and skills that can enable them to improve their lives. Besides, it also stresses on the need for basic services, social development strategies, income-generation measures and legal protection for children, their families and communities.[27]

UNICEF, established in 1946 on a voluntary basis, began as a temporary relief operation mainly in Europe. By 1953, its mandate to work exclusively in the developing world became firmly established. The US government is UNICEF's largest donor. Every year the UNICEF has to go to governments for financial support, and particularly to the US Government.

The elimination of child labour, especially hazardous one, a priority concern of the ILO and of UNICEF, now needs to become the world's shared and urgent goal. The UNICEF puts emphasis on the need for collective action in order to deal with the problem of child labour. The economic exploitation of the children will be protected / stopped only when the governments, international and national organizations and all members of the world community, work together.

So far as the objectives of UNICEF is concerned, we see that the main focus of UNICEF has been on the compulsory prevention of child labour through primary education. In addition to this, it has provided financial and technical support for legal enforcement, studies on child labour, and workshops and discussion on the problem at the national and state levels. It aims at promoting convergence of all sectoral and development programmes on "at risk" families for prevention of child labour and wants to strengthen monitoring systems on child labour. It further aims to assist central and state governments to develop and implement programmes and action plans for the release and rehabilitation of children from labour in various industries and occupations. More recently, the UNICEF has been involved in combating child trafficking and prostitution by organizing regional workshops and is working with the National Human Rights Commission to coordinate policy action and advocacy.[28] It was recognized that the UNICEF should play a major role within the UN system for street children, but in terms of actions should, 'concentrate mainly on advocacy and rely primarily on governments and voluntary agencies for implementation'.[29] Advocacy was therefore seen as UNICEF's natural role and advantage while the more sensitive campaigning work should be left to NGOs.[30]

Over the years, the international approach to children has changed dramatically. The initial idea that children have special needs has given way to the conviction that children have same set of rights which the adults have. These rights are civil and political, social, cultural and economic and are termed as human rights. Since child labour has been treated as a human rights issue, it becomes pertinent to point out the various United Nations pronouncements on human rights relating to child labour. These pronouncements are:

- The Universal Declaration of Human Rights, 1948

- The International Covenant on Human Rights, 1966.
- The Supplementary Convention on the Abolition of Slavery, 1956.
- The Convention for the Suppression of the Traffic in Persons and of the Exploitation of the Prostitution of others, 1949.
- The Declaration of the Rights of the Child, 1959.

In order to take up the human rights dimension of child labour, effectively, the NGOs have lobbied United Nations agencies (particularly UNICEF) to pay more attention to the issue.[31] UNICEF's Draft Working Paper for its 1986 Executive Board recommended that UNICEF should work to enhance government and public awareness of children in especially difficult circumstances and of possibilities for preventive and ameliorative actions.[32]

The belief that children possess rights as adults has been expressed as the Convention on the rights of the child. It has now been ratified by all except a few countries. Once ratified, it becomes the duty of the governments to protect children from exploitation and from performing any work that is likely to be hazardous or to interfere with the child's education, or to be harmful to the child's health or physical, mental, spiritual, moral or social development.[33]

The Convention on the rights of the child is as important for tackling the children as the Constitution is for the country. It has facilitated conversion of the basic needs of the children into their normative rights. It is a landmark document by which the children have been empowered and an environment has been created in which all children are able to live securely and realize their full potential. The responsibility of implementing the convention lies with all those concerned with children.

The twin movements on behalf of children — one based on 'rights' and the other on 'needs' have come together and formed one whole. The 'rights' approach focuses on those who are disadvantaged by denial of specific legally constituted rights. But reaching children with 'basic needs' — under the terms of the convention on the rights of the child - target a virtually identical group. Those who are disadvantaged by unmet rights and those who are disadvantaged by unmet needs are ultimately the same children.

UNICEF and its many partners have played a vital role in the children's movement. Without their championing, the children's cause could not have been propelled to its current high levels of visibility and policy commitment.

Children do a variety of work in widely divergent conditions and this work can become exploitative also especially when child labour involves:

- full time work at too early an age;
- too many hours spent working;
- work that leads to undue physical, social or psychological stress;
- inadequate pay and too much responsibility;
- work in bad conditions;
- work as a slave or bonded labour;
- work that hampers access to education; and
- work that retards full social and psychological development.

Even the UNICEF has found these works to be exploitative as it retards the full development of the child's personality and does not give him a chance to study. UNICEF expressed this view during the late eighties and early nineties.

These exploitative kinds of work endangers child's development from the following angles:

- Physical development — including overall health, coordination, strength, vision and hearing;
- Cognitive development — including literacy, numeracy and the acquisition of knowledge necessary to normal life;
- Emotional development — including adequate self-esteem, family attachment, feelings of love and acceptance;
- Social and moral development — including a sense of group identity, the ability to cooperate with others and the capacity to distinguish right from wrong.[34]

Besides, they are also vulnerable psychologically. They suffer devastating psychological damage especially in an environment where they work as slaves or bonded labour and where their self-esteem and dignity is undermined.

All these sufferings and exploitation can be taken care of with the help of education. Education helps a child develop cognitively, emotionally and socially. UNICEF believes that education can be taken to child workers more directly.

When we talk about the causes of child labour, UNICEF points out that child exploitation is not an accident, rather it is done purposely. In certain industries, like the carpet industry and in electronic assemblies, children are employed because of the dexterity of their small fingers.

UNICEF has evolved two approaches towards improving the lives of working children viz. i) using legal instruments to limit and define the conditions under which children work; and ii) transforming the nature of work itself.

The legal instrument which has been used to limit or prohibit child labour is the adoption of Minimum Age Convention which fixed the minimum age of work at 14 years. Many countries have laws and regulations prohibiting, limiting or regulating child labour as it is notorious, though these laws are implemented more in their breach. Another way in which legal intervention is made is by providing equal pay for equal work, regulating the weekly rest day, etc.

In case of the second one, i.e. transforming the nature of work itself, education is an important component. Under this approach, the basic thrust is on improving the basic services, health care, nutrition and education being made available to the community as a whole, as well as special programmes directed specially to working children.

So far as UNICEF India's position is concerned, it aims to abolish child labour within a specified period of time in a phased manner. The UNICEF India policy on child labour is given below.

All forms of child labour should be eliminated to comply with agreed child rights.

The enactment and enforcement of legislation to make primary education compulsory is a pre-requisite for the elimination of child labour.

The modification and enforcement of existing legislation on child labour is a necessary, supportive measure for the elimination of child labour.

UNICEF seeks to strengthen non-governmental alliances which are effective in drawing public attention to the issue and generating social mobilization for the elimination of child labour.

It focuses on programmes to rehabilitate children released

from labour into the educational system and to improve the livelihoods of their families through support from anti-poverty programmes.[35]

UNICEF India in their Position Paper on Child Labour stated that there is a major shift in policy and commitment towards the elimination of child labour. While it is true that child labour has strongly arisen as an issue on the Indian political agenda because of national and international campaigning, there is certainly no strong commitment yet on the part of the Central and most State Governments to really tackle child labour and invest in the education of working children in a massive way. The recent report, 'status of working children in the country; initiatives for their education; challenges for the future',[36] of the Department of Education, shows this ambiguity. The report concludes that there are different views on the approach to child labour. One view holds that 'educational facilities should be provided to working children outside their hours of work', whereas the other view holds that 'children must be withdrawn from work and be allowed to become part of the formal school system'. A choice between these two views is however not made.

UNICEF advocates a comprehensive strategy against hazardous child labour including compulsory education for children and employment for parents. UNICEF's overall strategy is based upon advocacy for government to adopt and pursue former policies to eliminate child labour and promote compulsory primary education and for industry itself to respond constructively to pressures to replace child with adult labour. The strategy further seeks to develop and strengthen new alliances with NGOs, industry, external agencies, media, academics and advocates, which may bring innovative approaches to bear on the removal of children from the work place.

Under the strategy regarding universalisation of primary education, UNICEF is willing to support the initiatives of State Governments to enforce compulsory primary education in districts of concentration of child labour. UNICEF facilitates the dissemination of successful NGO experiences in removing children from the work place and integrating them into the school system, through training, workshops and field visits.

So far UNICEF's strategy regarding legislation is concerned, UNICEF advocates for revision of Child Labour Act, as it has certain loopholes, and suggests that government should introduce more rigorous enforcement procedures.

UNICEF not only talks about strategies like compulsory primary education and legislation. It also talks about public awareness. Press coverage on the plight of child labourer is growing day by day and it is visible not only in India but also abroad. UNICEF provides and will continue to provide reliable information to the media. Besides, a parallel initiative has been established to promote national awareness and action on the Child Rights Convention through information disseminations, NGO activities, state-wise schemes and activities to mobilize children.

Another area where the UNICEF is involved, is the monitoring and research activities. Monitoring is basically done by the Child Labour Cell which is functioning at the National Labour Institute. UNICEF supports the Child Labour Cell for monitoring and research activities and explores ways by which the monitoring function at the national, state and district levels can be strengthened.

Besides all these, UNICEF provides assistance for the development of inter-sectoral programmes for the release and rehabilitation of child labourers. This is done with the help of UNICEF State Offices.

Apart from the ILO and UNICEF, there are some other UN agency supported programmes that are increasingly concerned with the child labour problem. They are the UNDP's South Asia Poverty Alleviation Programme, UNDCP Programme for street children, UNESCO's Learning Without Frontiers of India's adult literacy programme, UNIFEM's entrepreneurship development programmes for women, and UNAIDS activities on child trafficking.[37] Even the World Bank has also started taking serious note of child labour in India as a development issue. The World Bank would support measures like reducing the demand for specific workers in specific sectors and in industries.

Summing Up

From the above discussion it becomes clear that both the ILO and the UNICEF have played a very significant role in combating child labour. The convention on the rights of the child is a landmark document and is the first legally binding global prescription to give to the children the best they deserve. Hence, creating awareness about the convention, is a necessity and calls for a joint effort of all those who are concerned with children. The International conferences on child labour, such as the Amsterdam (February 1997), Oslo (October 1997), and the Stockholm Conferences are examples of growing global initiatives aimed at mobilizing world public opinion against it.

The National Child Labour laws must accord with both the spirit and letter of the convention and with relevant ILO convention. Such legislation must encompass the vast minority of child work in the informal sector of the economy including work on the streets and forms, domestic work or work within the child's own household. The ILO should take steps to encourage the effective cooperation of all agencies concerned with the elimination of exploitation of child labour, and in particular establish a framework for improved liaison between Governments, voluntary organizations, trade unions, employers and families of working children. The NGOs have become an increasingly powerful force and as such should take more effective action against child labour.

REFERENCES

1. Mishra, Lakshmidhar, Child Labour in India, Oxford University Press, New Delhi, 2000, 184.
2. World of Work, the Magazine of ILO, No. 4, Bureau of Public Information of the ILO, Geneva, 1993, p. 4.
3. Devi, Laxmi, Encyclopaedia of Family and Child Welfare, Vol. 4, Institute for Sustainable Development, Lucknow and Anmol Publications, New Delhi, 1998, p. 72.
4. Child Labour, A Briefing Manual, International Labour Office, Geneva, 1986, p. 14.
5. World of Work, op. cit., p. 74.
6. Verma, A.K., "Child Labour in India", in Manpower Journal, Vol. XXI, No. I, April-June, 1985, p. 95.
7. Kulshrestha, Jinesh Chandra, Indian Child Labour, Uppal Publishing House, New Delhi, 1994, pp. 92-93.
8. Report of the 57th Session of the International Labour Conference, Geneva, 1972, p. 5.
9. Fyfe, Alec, Child Labour, Polity Press, U.K., 1989, p. 131.
10. Ibid., p. 132.
11. Mishra, Lakshmidhar, op.cit., pp. 185-188.

12. Ibid.
13. Fyfe, Alec, op.cit., p. 133.
14. Kulshreshtha, Jinesh Chandra, op.cit., p. 102.
15. Joseph, M.P., IPEC in India Looking Back, New Delhi, 1992-95.
16. International Labour Review, Vol. 136, No. 2, ILO Office, Geneva, 1997, p. 245.
17. IPEC Filer, International Labour Office, Geneva.
18. IPEC, Reflection on the Past, Pointers to the Future, ILO Office, Geneva, 1994, p. 4.
19. Mishra, Lakshmidhar, op.cit., pp. 235-36.
20. International Labour Review, op.cit., p. 249.
21. IPEC, op.cit., p. 5.
22. IPEC Filer, op.cit.
23. Mishra, Lakshmidhar, op.cit., p. 237.
24. Ibid.
25. IPEC Filer, op.cit.,
26. International Labour Review, op.cit., p. 250.
27. Summary of UNICEF's The State of the World's Children, Oxford University Press, 1996.
28. Mishra, Lakshmidhar, op.cit., p. 238.
29. UNICEF, Informal Paper by Chairman of the Executive Board, New York, 1986, p. 3.
30. Fyfe, Alec, op.cit., p. 136.
31. Ibid.
32. UNICEF, Children in Especially Difficult Circumstances, Unpublished paper for the Executive Board 1986 Session, New York, 1986, p. 14.
33. The State of the World's Children, Published for UNICEF by Oxford University Press, 1997, p. 17.
34. Bequele, A. and Myers, W.E., First things first in Child Labour:Eliminating Work Detrimental to Children, UNICEF/ILO, Geneva, 1995, pp. 6-7.
35. Awards Digest, Journal of Labour Legislation, Vol. XX, No. 7-12, July — December, 1994.
36. Bhattacharya, Sheba, Child Labour and Education Case Study in Delhi, APPPA Dissertation, Indian Institute of Public Administration, New Delhi, 2002-03, pp. 49-50 (Unpublished).
37. Mishra, Lakshmidhar, op.cit., p. 238

4

Government and NGO's Concern for Child Labour

Child Labour, a social problem, needs positive, constructive and timely intervention by experts, government and NGO's with adequate supportive services supplementing the family income. Ever since Independence in 1947, the Government of India has been concerned with child labour and has followed a proactive policy in handling this problem. The Indian Constitution, under the Directive Principles of State Policy, has provided certain provisions prohibiting employment of children. The essence of Government's policy is that all working children are also children and must be given the opportunities to develop into healthy well-rounded personalities.

Government's Concern

The Government's concern for child labour became visible with the setting up of a 16 member Committee on Child Labour in 1979. The committee was headed by M.S. Gurupadaswamy and was to inquire into the causes leading to and problems arising out of employment of children and also to suggest measures by which we could protect the children. The Committee drew up a plan of action for the conduct of in-depth and diagnostic studies on the nature and extent of the problem of adequacy of the existing legal framework and the supportive measures for working children.

The Committee was of the view that a distinction had to be drawn between child labour and its exploitation. The Committee further viewed that:

'labour becomes an absolute evil in the case of the child when he is required to work beyond his physical capacity, when hours of employment interfere with his education, recreation and rest, when the wages are not commensurate with quantum of work done and when the occupation he is engaged endangers his health and safety.'[1]

The Committee submitted its report in December 1979. Some of the recommendations of the Committee are:[2]

i) The existing laws relating to prohibition and regulation of employment of children should be consolidated into a single comprehensive code in order to prevent any ambiguity in respect of the basic objectives.
ii) In case of child workers, the periodical medical check-ups should be linked up with the National Health Scheme.
iii) In the areas where there may be concentration of working children, arrangements should be made for non-formal education.
iv) In the areas, where there are large number of working children, recreational and cultural activities should be provided.

These aspects of the problem were considered by the Ministry of Labour. It felt that there is a need to ensure the health and safety of children at the workplace and that they should be protected from excessively long working hours and from night work.

The seventh five-year plan (1985-90), approved by the National Development Council, said that since it is not feasible to eradicate Child Labour, the government should try to make the conditions of working children more acceptable. The plan proposed a greater role for voluntary agencies in providing child workers with health care, nutrition and education. The abolition of child labour, it said, could only be achieved when there is sufficient improvement in the conditions of the families whose children are compelled to work.[3] Keeping these points in view, the Government adopted a new set of policies i.e., National Child Labour Policy in 1987 which comprised of a legislative action plan; focusing general development programmes to benefit child labour and project based action plans in areas of high concentration of child labour engaged in wage/quasi-wage employment.

The entry of the Government of India into ILO's IPEC programme in 1992 indicated the Government's growing concern about child labour and the need to act against it. The advent of

IPEC in India coincided with government initiatives to tackle the problem systematically. These included the historic declaration made by the then Prime Minister, Shri P.V. Narasimha Rao, on August 15, 1994.[4] This was the first major political announcement on release of children from hazardous work and rehabilitation of such children. The Prime Minister also announced Rs. 850 crores fund to be administered over the next five years on schemes for the elimination of child labour in hazardous industries. The Prime Minister's statement is an unequivocal demonstration of the Government's concern about the deep rooted malady of child labour and its determination and commitment to overcome it.[5]

A National Authority on Elimination of Child Labour was constituted under the Chairmanship of Union Labour Minister with Secretaries of nine Departments of Government of India concerned with Child Labour to oversee the implementation of schemes using the fund. A comprehensive programme of action was drawn up to release two million children employed in hazardous nature of work by 2002 A.D. A Conference of 62 district collectors was held in September, 1995, to give a final shape to the Action Plan. Finally, 76 projects were sanctioned in 76 districts to translate the plan to action known as National Child Labour Projects.[6]

The period 1992-95 marked a turning point in the country's perspective on child labour. The impetus for the change came from the increasing media attention on the issue, spurred by the work done by NGOs. But the most important was the clear direction the government took, focusing on a phased elimination of child labour.[7]

In India, there have been several legislation — both before and after independence - which are mainly directed to restrict the minimum age of children at the time of employment in certain type of work, as well as to regulate the working conditions. Many enquiry commissions have been constituted by the Government to look into the problem and suggest remedial measures to ameliorate the problems of working children. Unfortunately, due to some reason or the other, all these efforts seem to have had very little impact on the incidence of child labour. The available data does not show any decline in number of child workers in general, not even in hazardous occupation.[8]

The Labour ministry has indicated that despite the provision of restrictive laws, the practice of child labour continues unabated, because exploitation of children is of financial advantage to employers and a matter of economic compulsion to parents. In its annual report (1983-84) the Ministry of Labour said that the government had accepted child labour as a "harsh reality" and that it was neither "feasible nor opportune" to prevent children from working in the present stage of economic development.[9] Under these circumstances, the Ministry proposed to take measures to improve the working conditions of children, rather than removing them from the work force. The National Child Labour Policy of 1987 were formulated in pursuance of this. This policy was not an adequate response to the 44 million children working in the country as it was only for 30,000 children in 10 project areas. However, it was a modest beginning towards the right end. Some steps have been taken to implement the project based plan of action through National Child Labour Projects (NCLPs).

The main thrust of the NCLP is to reduce the incidence of child labour in the project areas thereby encouraging the elimination of child labour progressively. Some of the activities of the NCLP are:[10]

i) Stepping up enforcement of child labour laws;
ii) Non-formal education;
iii) Adult education;
iv) Income and employment generation;
v) Special schools;
vi) Raising public awareness; and
vii) Survey and evaluation.

The principal agency for implementation of these were project societies which were formed and registered under the Registration of Societies Act, 1860. The actual implementation of various schemes under the project are being carried out by local NGOs.

Elimination of child labour needs an effective mechanism to provide inputs for policy formulations and programme support. Keeping this in mind, a Child Labour Cell was set up in 1990 in the V.V. Giri National Labour Institute. In response to the need for augmenting the activities of the Cell and to meet demands of different interest groups engaged in the elimination of the child labour, the Cell was upgraded to the National Resource Centre on

Child Labour (NRCCL). The NRCCL was set up in March 1993 to assist national and state governments, NGOs, policy makers, legislators and social groups through a variety of interventions and to develop capabilities of the target groups. The NRCCL gets financial support from the Ministry of Labour, Government of India and UNICEF.

It has built up an impressive and one of the largest documentation on child labour and is now assisting the Ministry of Labour in the implementation of child labour projects. The NRCCL has set two kinds of goals for itself. The long term goal includes to establish Regional Network Centres and to identify partners in Asian Countries. The Centre's short term goal is to establish Centres in States with high concentration of Child Labour.[11] Research and training are the two important activities of the NRCCL. Besides these two activities, the NRCCL performs a number of other activities like documentation and dissemination, publication, workshops, seminars, networking, etc.

So far as the research activity is concerned, it revolves around updating and upgrading the existing information as well as exploring new aspects related to child labour. The training activity involves bringing about an attitudinal change in the trainees to enable them to play the role of agents of change. The training programmes are participatory in nature and seek to create greater awareness on the nature, magnitude and dimensions of the problem of child labour. While imparting training, care is taken to design the training in such a way that it meets the requirements of different target groups of trainees. Besides the normal training programmes, the Centre also conducts the training of Trainers programme, which aims at creating a larger pool of trainers for achieving wider coverage.

The Centre provides technical support services to various agencies like Trade Unions, Non-Governmental Organizations, Universities, and others engaged in the implementation of Child Labour Projects. The Centre lays special emphasis on organizing workshops and seminars which helps in catalyzing new and innovative programmes and actions. These workshops/seminars are meant for people belonging to diverse groups such as NGOs, trade unions, labour and factory inspectors, district collectors and Project Directors, film makers, training institutes, etc.

Yet another activity of the Centre is dissemination of

information through its number of publications. Besides, the Centre has been working in close collaboration with international agencies, like ILO and UNICEF, State Labour institutes, NGOs, trade unions, employers organizations and judiciary. The Centre has established a network with about 400 NGOs in assisting them through various ways of implementing child labour programmes.

Apart from the NRCCL, the Institute has set up a legal studies cell in September 1997, with a view to provide legal support services on child labour to national and state governments, policy makers, legislators and social groups. The main activities of the Cell are:[12]

i) To review the existing child labour laws;
ii) To conduct training on legal aspects of child;
iii) To examine the structure of enforcement system on child labour;
iv) To collect, analyse and disseminate information on judgements, orders and laws relating to child labour;
v) To provide legal support to prosecute or take on appeal a few cases relating to violation of laws on child labour.

After looking into the measures taken by the Government, one can say that Government alone cannot achieve success as the problem pertaining to child labour is quite a complex one. Government will have to take the help and active cooperation from other concerned quarters by ensuring active involvement of experts, activists, planners, administrators and above all NGOs already working in the area of the child labour. Though the government has already started working actively on the above lines, yet it is desirable on its part to associate all these people consistently from its inception to the conclusion of the action programme. Training may be imparted to officials and NGOs working in the areas of child labour.

In order to integrate any work concerned on child with the national agenda, it is essential to have close interaction with state Governments. This interaction has to take place, not merely at the national policy-making tier but at many levels. The contours of the national policy on child labour are set by the views, opinions and pressures surfacing from below. As such, it becomes necessary to work in close cooperation of government bodies at the bottom tiers as well, especially in the states and districts.

NGO's Concern

The problem of child labour in the country is so complex that the State alone cannot tackle it. The NGOs support is required to supplement State's effort. The State may profit from the experiences and the experiments of the NGOs. With regard to child labour, a large number of NGOs have been playing supplementary and complementary roles to the State.

The NGOs are independent of statutory authority and their policies are framed and controlled by their own members. The thoughts and actions of these NGOs aim at the creation of such a society where good life shall be possible for all.[13] NGOs are neither government contractors, nor substitutes for government, nor competitors of governmental action. NGOs are important partners and collaborators of government and should be viewed as such.[14] They generally organize themselves at various levels as groups and are prepared to accept responsibility for social action and to devote time and energies to achieve their objectives by means of democratic social action outside the machinery of government. They try to bring about a structural transformation and social revolution.[15]

NGOs play an important role in the elimination of child labour. The common features in their programmes are that they have health and nutrition components, non-formal education, vocational training, recreational facilities. Some of them even have counseling and saving schemes.

Since the International Year of the Child, NGOs have become an increasingly powerful force, lobbying the UN system to adhere to the principles enshrined in the various UN pronouncements, and to take more effective action against child labour. NGOs like the Anti-Slavery Society, have produced some of the best documented country studies of child labour. Some other NGOs like the Geneva-based Defence for Children International have taken up the human rights dimension of child labour.[16]

These examples show that not only in India, but world over, NGOs are actively involved in the elimination of child labour. In case of India, some NGOs are based in urban and semi-urban centers while some others in rural areas. They are working both for the integrated development of children and the elimination of child labour. Some NGOs are working towards removal of working children completely from their work by training them in alternative skills, while some others are working towards improving the living and working conditions of the children.

The NGOs work not only for the elimination of child labour but also towards universalisation of elementary education in India. Some of the NGOs working in this direction are Lok Jumbish based in Rajasthan, M.V. Foundation in Andhra Pradesh, Ekalavya in Madhya Pradesh and CREDA in Uttar Pradesh. Besides these, there are some other NGOs like Theatre Action Group, Indian Council for Child Welfare (ICCW) and Butterflies, all Delhi based, which are working with street children. Still another group of NGOs like SEWA, Ankur, Delhi Council for Child Welfare (DCCW), Prabhatara, etc., are working primarily with working children. These NGOs differ from one another in their philosophies, approaches and strategies and their implementation strategies also differ. The working of some of the NGOs has been discussed below.

The M.V. Foundation, located in Ranga Reddy District of Andhra Pradesh, was established in 1981 and works with the objective of elimination of child labour. According to the M.V. Foundation, a child labour is one who is not part of the school system. This is regardless of whether the children are engaged in wage work or non-wage work, are self-employed or working for others; are engaged in hazardous or non-hazardous occupations; are earning a daily wage or are employed on a contract basis. So far as the funding is concerned, the foundation has a unique method, i.e., every month a nominal amount on each ration card is collected. The accumulated money is known as School Development Fund and it provides infrastructure like school buildings, benches and black boards for the education of the child labourers in the area. The foundation does not encourage Non Formal Education (NFE).[17] According to Shantha Sinha, of M.V. Foundation, its greatest failure is in its assumption that working children cannot be withdrawn from work while the fact, that there is an unfulfilled demand for formal education even among poor in rural areas has been totally denied.[18]

The M.V. Foundation project had its impact on the children, the parents, the youth, the village/mandal panchayats etc.[19] So far as the children are concerned, they are no longer working, rather they are studying. Those children who have been withdrawn from work and are studying, are acting as resource persons in the campaign against child labour. With regards to parents, we find a change in their attitude in the sense that now they are willing to invest in their education and are no longer dependent on their earnings. In case of Panchayats, they are vying with one another to free their villages of child labour and bonded labour. Secondly, they are trying to improve school facilities and also giving priority to schools in the allocation of funds.

Another NGO working towards universalisation of elementary education is the Rajasthan based Lok Jumbish,[20] which encourages people's participation and works towards the empowerment of women through education. Lok Jumbish has initiated Sahej Shiksha (non-formal education) which is different from the mainstream NFF system.

Under this programme, a child is allowed to learn at his/her own pace. These kind of schools have been established in those areas where schools do not exist or where teachers do not go regularly due to distances. These programmes are funded by SIDA, central and state governments.

Arunodhaya, a NGO, established in 1942, in Chennai, is a centre for working children and works for the cause of child workers. The basic objective of this centre is to work towards changing the hazardous and exploitative situation of child workers and to provide protection and assistance to those child labourers who have been victims of various forms of abuse and exploitation.[21] It also works towards promoting alternative education which is helpful in empowering the child workers. Besides, it also aims at providing additional support system for the families of child workers which will ensure quality life and an environment conducive to the proper development of children.

Arunodhaya runs special schools, where children are trained by the staff of the NGO and once they get equipped with the lessons, they are enrolled into the formal school by the NGO. These special schools are run with the aid provided by the Child Relief and You (CRY) and the ILO. After enrolling the child labourers into the formal school system, the NGO keeps a check on them in the sense that whether they are attending the formal school regularly or not. For this, the centre conducts tuitions for them in the seven tuition centres which has been organized by the organization.

Butterflies programme for street children (Delhi),[22] began its programme in February 1988. They started their work with destitute street children and later on expanded it to include coolie boys of INA market and the street vendors and shoe blacks at Connaught Place as also the street girl children. Butterflies has a non-formal education programme, recreational activities and a saving scheme. Those boys who were school drop-outs were motivated to join the open school.

The Centre for Rural Education and Development Action (CREDA) was founded in 1982 and has been fighting child and bonded child labour. It has been conducting a wide range of activities in this area with active and widespread support from members of the local community. In 1992, when the IPEC and CLASP were initiated in India, CREDA was identified to implement some components of both. In order to eliminate child labour, CREDA has adopted the following stratgegy.[23]

i) CREDA took the initiative in withdrawing working children from carpet looms, admitting them in the special schools, providing them with midday meals, arranging stipends for the children, and opening bank accounts for each child.

ii) CREDA's most important strategy was community mobilization through face to face interaction with individuals and groups. Through this interaction an awareness was created about the negative effects of making children work on carpet looms. A few activists were identified by CREDA in each village who were keen to work with it as volunteers.

iii) Another important strategy adopted by CREDA was advocacy which was undertaken on a massive scale extending from parents to neighbours, loom owners, carpet manufacturers and exporters, adult weavers, members of the village community/panchayat, working children, school children, though with varying frequency and impact.

iv) As a part of its educational strategy, CREDA made special efforts not only to enroll girls into its own schools for child labour (special schools under the NCLP) but in addition motivated parents to enroll their girls in the regular government schools.

So far as the impact of CREDA's project activities is concerned, we see that it has left an impact on the various sections of the society. It has organized women into self-help groups through savings and credit. Due to CREDA's activities, there has been a substantial reduction of child labour in the carpet industry. The village leaders are of the view that if CREDA had not come for help, then the children would have continued to work behind the looms. CREDA was successful in spreading the message of gender sensitization in the project area, creating an awareness in the community of the importance of educating girls. With the efforts of CREDA, an end was put to the painful nine hour work day and grauelling seven days a week routine which was followed at the looms. It also introduced a remarkable quality of punctuality, discipline, and hygiene for thousands of children liberated from the looms and enrolled in the special schools.

Asha Nivas, a registered NGO, initiated in 1976, works for the marginalized and exploited children residing in Chennai. The main objective of this includes: sponsorship and scholarship for education of the working children; continuing education for school drop-outs; non-formal education and vocational training for working children; shelter homes for working children; recreational activities; health care and health education programmes; etc.[24] The prime concept that is realized through this programme is retaining children in school and preventing them from becoming child workers. Thirty continuing education centers have been started to prepare the drop-outs for government exams. Shelter homes provides family atmosphere for children to grow towards change. Non-formal education, recreation facilities and health services are regular feature of the shelter home.

Besides all these, development programmes are implemented for child workers to rehabilitate them by the NGO in Chennai City slums. People living in the slums are made aware about the evils of child labour. Medical check up is provided for the child labourers at regular intervals to ensure normal childhood by the organization.

Ruchika Social Service Wing[25] was established in 1985-86 and targeted children who work on the platforms of the railway stations. The Bhubaneswar railway station and nine-other nearby stations were targeted in the first phase of the project which lasted for eighteen months. NFE centres were set up on the railway platform itself and the children working in and around the stations were encouraged to attend the classes that were held each day for only two or three hours. After attending these classes, the children continued with their work for the rest of the day. An important component of the programme was counseling and sensitizing the parents on the importance of education.

After completion of 18 months, the second stage of the programme started. A three-tier strategy was developed for school enrolment. The children, around 300, who were attending the NFE centres were to be shifted to full time day centres located near the railway stations. In these day centres, emphasis was to be laid on academic side with a view to mainstreaming the brighter of the children into the formal school system. Finally, an attempt would be made to gradually wear the children away from work towards full-time education, with the help of education, regular mid day meals, health services, etc.

So far as the impact of this programme is concerned, it was heartening to note that in the first year of project itself, sixty working children were withdrawn from the workforce and admitted to regular schools. The children were happy with the content and quality of the educational programme as well as the support services (health, hygiene, nutrition, etc.) provided to them. Besides, they were empowered to use the post-office, banks, and other facilities.

Summing Up

The working of the various NGOs across the country shows that the NGOs are really showing enthusiasm and dedication in identifying and releasing children from work and in rehabilitating them. The NGOs are working for the philosophy that all the working children should be in regular day school and that the government school system will only start functioning and improving if enough community pressure is built up to make it function. The Government has tended to take refuge in adhoc supplementary programmes such as NFE, Operation Blackboard and the national mid-day meal scheme. Some of these programmes have met localized success but on the whole, they have fallen short of expectations for want of political backing.[26] In case of Operation Blackboard which was started in 1987 and which targeted to provide an additional teacher to the single teacher schools, to construct an additional class-room for these schools and to provide them with essential teaching material, the parliamentary committee on education found 'the ground reality to be quite different' ranging from slow progress in the construction and utilization of new classrooms to reluctance of newly appointed teachers to work in rural areas.[27]

An NGO forum plays a vital role in dealing with working children. With the coordinated efforts of NGOs working for the same cause in a given city, there is a great scope to work in the areas of orientation, awareness-building and empowerment of children. A large number of NGOs have come into existence and have helped to build a basic infrastructure of educational, health and economic services for the child labourers. The NGOs have undertaken highly innovative, cost-effective and result oriented initiatives in a few pockets of the country and produced striking results. Still the fact remains that in terms of coverage or spread this is negligible and uneven.[28]

To conclude, we can say that a single individual or a group or one agency alone cannot solve the problem of child labour. A multi-pronged approach is required. Over the years, the government has gradually shifted the responsibility onto the NGOs. The NGOs are being invited to take over and implement various social welfare programmes primarily because NGO strategies and approach are effective and low cost. Thus, it becomes even more important that NGOs form a strong alliance, an alliance that believes in the right of the child to survival, protection, development, growth, participation and freedom of expression. Besides NGOs, the government can seek the assistance of various private agencies which would be willing to help.

REFERENCES

1. Mishra, Lakshmidhar, Child Labour in India, Oxford University Press, New Delhi, 2000, p. 195.
2. Kulshreshtha, Jinesh Chandra, Indian Child Labour, Uppal Publishing House, New Delhi, 1994, pp. 85-86.
3. Weiner, Myron, The Child and the State in India, Oxford University Press, New Delhi, 1991, p. 83.

4. Doval, N.K., "Double — Speak on Child Labour", in The Hindu, December 28, 1994, p. 14.
5. "PM Wants Time-bound End to Child Labour', in The Hindu, September 15, 1995, p. 3.
6. Child Labour Law — An Overview, Child Labour Legal Studies Cell, V.V. Giri National Labour Institute, Noida, 1998, p. 35.
7. Joseph, M.P., IPEC in India 1992-95, Looking Back, International Labour Organisation, New Delhi, 1996, p. 2.
8. Pati, R.N., Rehabilitation of Child Labour in India, Ashish Publishing House, New Delhi, p. 269.
9. Government of India, Ministry of Labour, Annual Report 1983-84, New Delhi, 1985.
10. Mishra, Lakshmidhar, Jain, Mahaveer and Mohsin, Nadeem, Report of National Seminar on Implementation of Child Labour Projects, Published by National Resource Centre on Child Labour, V.V. Giri National Labour Institute, Noida, 1997, p. 3.
11. Child Labour Law — An Overview, op.cit., p. 212.
12. Ibid., p. 214.
13. Sachchidananda, "Voluntary Agencies and Challenge of Eighties", in Journal of Social and Economic Studies, Vol IX, No. 2, 1981, pp. 149-50.
14. Mishra, Laskmidhar, op.cit., p. 271.
15. Ibid., p. 150.
16. Fyfe, Alec, Child Labour, Polity Press, UK, 1989, p. 136.
17. Bhargava, Pramila H., The Elimination of Child Labour whose Responsibility?, Sage Publications, New Delhi, 2003, pp. 119-20.
18. Bhattacharya, Sheba, Child Labour and Education, Case Study in Delhi, APPPA Dissertation, Indian Institute of Public Administration, New Delhi, 2002-03, p. 42 (Unpublished).
19. Mishra, Lakshmidhar, op.cit., pp. 281-82.
20. Bhargava, Pramila H., op.cit., p. 120.
21. Brochure of Arunodhaya Social Service Centre, Chennai.
22. Working and Street Children in Delhi, National Labour Institute, Noida.
23. Mishra, Lakshmidhar, op.cit., pp. 283-86.
24. Annual Report of Asha Nivas Social Service Centre, Chennai, 1996-97, p. 2.
25. Mishra, Lakshmidhar, op.cit., pp. 287-89.
26. Bhattacharya, Sheba, op.cit., p. 43.
27. Times of India, July 21, 1998.
28. Mishra, Lakshmidhar, op.cit., p. 321.

5

Child Labour in Delhi

India claims to be the largest democracy and independent country in the world, yet 55 million children are working in India. Delhi has the largest number of child workers in India. One of the causes of Child Labour in India, according to Prayas, is the trend of rural to urban migration and migration from smaller towns to bigger cities. A large number of people migrate to Delhi in search for work and the availability of better job opportunities. Some people are forced to move out of their native place because of natural calamities like floods, famines, etc. As a result, more than two-thirds of working children are migrants, who have migrated mainly from the nearby Hindi speaking areas of Uttar Pradesh, Bihar, Rajasthan, Madhya Pradesh, etc.

Normally, the working children belong to the larger families, who consider them an economic asset rather than a liability in their struggle against poverty. About one-third of the working children belong to families with nine or more children.

Children start working in family undertaking from an early age along side their parents. They help their father in petty jobs on the streets, that too, without payment. Later on they are taken to their future employers by their parents, relatives or friends. Thus, they start to work on their own or for somebody else. These children are involved in various kinds of work like selling magazines and newspapers, selling fruits and peanuts, domestic and shop servants, working as rag pickers, polishing shoes, cleaning cars, begging, working at dhabas, etc.

In this introductory background, an attempt has been made to study the nature and condition of work in which the children in Delhi are involved. Besides, an attempt has also been made to highlight the efforts of the NGOs in improving the conditions of working children. But before proceeding to the nature and conditions of work, an attempt has been made to study the types of working children as also the difference between child work and child labour.

Types of Working Children

According to Prayas, all children who are out of school can be placed in the category of child labourers or potential child labourers. They may fall in either of the following categories:

i) Children working within regular employment conditions and contract;
ii) Children in self-employment in both formal and non-formal sectors;
iii) Children in conditions of bondage formal or informal; and
iv) Children working as part of their family labour.

Education wise, working children can be divided into three groups.[1]

In the first group, those children are included who do not and have never been to school. The second group comprises of those who had joined school and studied for few years but later on left the school because they had started working. The last group contains those children who work as well as spend a few hours in school everyday. In case of India, most of the working children fall in the first group. The reasons for this has already been discussed in the second chapter. In most of the developing countries having more children is considered as an asset because every child means two extra hands to work. In other words, more income for the family.

From an another angle, child labour can again be divided into three groups. In the first group those children are included who, a large number of them, particularly the young girls, help their parents in domestic work. Domestic work includes — harvesting and thrashing in the farms; collecting fuel and water, looking after the younger siblings; doing the household chores like cooking, cleaning, dusting, sweeping, etc. These works are considered as domestic work and falls in the first category of child labour.

In the second group comes those children who are made to learn family arts and crafts at a very young age so that they become proficient in a job which would be a source of income to them when they gain adulthood. If this work is imposed upon the child, against his wishes, then it becomes exploitative in nature and can be no longer considered as work but labour. This work includes the participation in the production of economic goods and services, including unpaid family work in an economic enterprise, as well as work for pay or profit.[2]

The third group comprises of those children who work on the streets. Prayas defines street children as those living on the streets for most of the day, viz. beggars, vendors, newspaper sellers, rag-pickers, car washers, etc. Most of the time, street children, many of whom have run away from their homes due to various reasons, are constantly under the strict vigil and threat of the criminals, drug addicts, police, etc. These street children are further divided into three groups. The first group comprises of those children who stay with their parents on the public pavements and have a direct and continuous contact with their families. The second group of children are called "children on the street." These children are the ones who have occasional family contact and spend their days and some of their nights on the streets and in public places. The third category of children do not have any family contact and are described as "children of the street." They include refugees, displaced persons, runaways and orphans.[3]

On the basis of this categorization, we can differentiate between child work and child labour. Child work is one which the child does in order to help his family. Besides work he can continue with his studies. On the other hand, child labour is exploitative in the sense that children are forced to do a particular job and cannot continue their studies. The nature of exploitation, which distinguishes between child work and child labour can be judged by the following criteria:[4]

i) starting full time work at too early an age;
ii) spending too many hours at work which prevents them from attending school because of the lack of time and excessive fatigue;
iii) work that results in excessive physical, social and psychological strain upon the child;
iv) working and living on the streets in unhealthy and dangerous conditions;
v) inadequate remuneration for work outside the family;

vi) work that does not facilitate the social and psychological development of the child; and

vii) inhibition of child's self-confidence and self-esteem as a result of negative attitude of the society.

Thus, it can be said that when children work long hours in arduous and often hazardous tasks, at low wages, and often in unhygienic worksites with hardly any facilities, they are being exploited. Hence it cannot be child work but child labour.

Child Labour in Delhi: The Statistical Profile

The child workers are spread throughout the National Capital Territory of Delhi. According to one of the estimates there are nearly 4 lakh child workers in Delhi, who comprise about 18 per cent of the child population of the National Capital Territory of Delhi. Out of them about 30,000 work in the 5,000 registered and 25,000 unregistered tea shops and dhabas; about 20,000 work in scooter and car repair shops, and approximately 30,000 children are working as shop assistants and about 40,000 work as labourers (agriculture, construction and coolies etc.) and nearly 1,00,000 work as domestic servants (full time/part-time).[5]

However, according to the census figures of 1991 there are 27,351 child workers in Delhi.[6] This includes 26,670 main workers[7] and 681 marginal workers.[8] About two-fifths are engaged in non-household industries, nearly one-seventh in trade and commerce and less than one-third in other services.

According to the South Asian Coalition on Child Servitude (SACCS), in Delhi, there are between 500,000 — 600,000 working children, and the number continues to grow as the city develops. Recent studies by SACCS estimate that there are 50,000 children working in tea shops and restaurants, 30,000 in car and motorbike repair shops, 50,000 working in various shops, 40,000 in agriculture and related occupations and 130,000 in domestic service. Approximately 80 per cent of child workers in Delhi are boys and well over half are illiterate.[9] In recent years, the number of street children, child beggars, child prostitutes and street vendors has increased rapidly and there are now an estimated 200,000 such children in Delhi.[10]

Occupation

So far as their occupation is concerned, it is found that 'maids and other house keeping services' is the most popular main occupation among children in the urban areas, followed by labourers. The other important occupations are working in dhabas and tea-stalls selling newspapers, shoe-shining, guarding parked cars, collection of rags, automobile and cycle repair shops. In case of maids and other house keeping services, collection of rags and selling newspapers, both the boys as well as girls are involved. But in case of vocations like dhabas and tea stalls, shoe-shining, guarding parked cars and automobile and cycle rapair shops, girls do not work.

As per the SACCS estimate, types of labour vary in the many areas of the capital. For example, in Connaught Place, children are employed as vendors, shoe-shine boys, shop assistants and prostitutes; in Motia Khan, children work in manufacturing cardboard boxes and rexine bags, also as domestic servants, shop assistants and in the nickel plating industry; in Karol Bagh children work in tea-stalls, shops, motor-repair workshops and as rag-pickers; in Naraina area, children work in tailoring, small manufacturing units, as beggars or domestic servants; in outer Delhi, children mainly work in farms and diaries, although children, can also be found in small industrial units producing copper wire, spare parts and furniture; in Trans Yamuna, working children are mainly found in domestic service, construction work or begging.

Problems and Hazards

The SACCS studies further highlight that children face a lot of hazards in their work. The shoe-shine boys and those employed in the brick kiln industries, are prone to asthma, bronchitis and tuberculosis. Those children who are involved in embroidery work suffer from serious vision difficulties. The rag-pickers are subject to scabies, tetanus and asthma and the scooter mechanics are prone to mechanical accidents.

Besides these hazards, the working place and the conditions in which they work is not good either. Most of the time, they work without sufficient light and air, in unhygienic conditions, with little or no ventilation. Accidents often occur at the worksites and there are usually no first aid facilities available. The body is busy working like machine. The number of hours spent in working varies considerably from 6 to 8 hours per day to even 12 or 14 hours. In works like roadside cafes/dhabas, workshops or domestic work, often there is no fixed hours at all. In Delhi, on a cold winter evening or in the hot summer afternoon, one sees these children braving the weather in their scanty clothes. [11]

In case of street children, there is no health security at all. The children are exposed to extreme weather conditions, traffic hazards, besides becoming victims of unhealthy habits like smoking, drinking, etc. Even when they are ill, they continue to work because the daily earnings are very important to meet their basic needs in life. Since they do not have any place to live, most of them either sleep on the pavements, in corridors or market places. Since they do not get proper diet, they suffer from malnutrition, hunger and some common diseases like anemia, tuberculosis, bronchitis and vitamin deficiency.

Areas of High Concentration

After going through the statistical details of the child labour, the types of work they are involved in, the working conditions and the problems faced by them, it becomes pertinent to know the areas in which they are highly concentrated. Accordingly, in the succeeding pages the areas of high concentration of child labourers and street children[12] have been discussed.

The Railway Stations

The first area of high concentration of working and street children is the railway station. Since most of them are migrants, having left their families and home as a result of poverty, the railway station is a best option to get a job as well as a place to live. Once they become familiar with the place and earn some money, they move out of the railway station and come to city.

A large number of working children can be found at the three railway stations viz., New Delhi, Old Delhi and Hazrat Nizammuddin. Initially they start working in small places like tea shops, dhabas, etc. While working here, they get wages as well as a place to live. Some of them opt for other jobs like porters, vendors, shoe-blacks, etc. Some of them are even found begging and collecting rags at the railway stations.

These children, especially thc porters, are harassed by the police because they are working as unlicensed porter. The policemen charge money from them and sometimes even take them to custody. Despite this harassment, they continue working at the stations because they find the stations very safe as a large number of people are present at the stations.

Areas in the Walled City of Old Delhi

The children working in these areas such as Jama Masjid, Chandni Chowk, Bara Hindu Rao etc. are engaged as helpers in shops, small workshops, as rag-pickers, and a good number of them as beggars mainly near the Jama Masjid area. Most of the establishments, particularly those which involves manufacturing processes, are located in the lanes and by-lanes in the residential-cum-business areas away from the main roads. In these establishments, works like electro-plating, book binding, metal carving, Zardi work is done. The children who are working here are migrants as well as the localites who stay nearby the walled city.

Inter State Bus Terminus (ISBT) and Surroundings

Like the railway station, the ISBT and the areas surrounding it, is another most suitable place for children to make an earning. The children in this area are employed as vendors, service boys, porters and shoe-shines. Here again most of the children are localites. Some of the girl children work as shop assistants, selling readymade garments and woolen clothes at the Tibetan Monastery.

Connaught Place

This area is a busy commercial complex where children make fast money. In this area the Hanuman Mandir is situated, which is again a place where child labourers are found in large numbers. Here some of the children work alongwith their family members. The most common site seen here is the young girls engaged in the job of applying henna (mehandi) on the palms and feet of the ladies. In this job, they earn a lot. During the festival time and marriage season, these girls make a lot of money. But for this they have to put extra labour i.e. they work till midnight without taking much rest.

Besides the mehandi job, the children here are employed as vendors, selling glass and lac bangles, flowers, garlands etc., shoe-shine boys and above all as beggars. Beggars in maximum number is seen here. These children are also involved in drug business. Some of them are themselves drug addicts and are often found stealing and snatching things from the devotees.

Yamuna Bazaar

The area near the Yamuna Bazaar, especially the Prachin Hanuman Mandir, is another place where we can find child labourers. As in the case of Hanuman Mandir, Connaught Place, here too, one can find drug addicts and children involved in drug business. These children also become victims at the hands of the police, who charge money from them as bribe. Besides the drug business, the children are involved in selling sweets, flowers, garlands, etc. shoe-shine, begging and even rag-picking.

Turkman Gate and the Surrounding Area

The area comprising Turkman Gate, Darya Ganj, Asaf Ali Road, Ram Lila Ground, is another place where street children are found in large numbers. The children in this area are employed in various activities like rickshaw pulling, working with scooter and car mechanics, barbers, selling newspapers and drug peddlers. Most of these children take refuge in the night shelter at the Turkman Gate. Some of them prefer the footpaths.

Trans Yamuna

In this area, there are a number of Jhuggi-jhopari camps which have been inhabited by the migrants. The children of this area work as domestic servants, rag pickers, construction workers and apprentices at tailoring shops. The hygienic condition in the jhuggi-jhopari area is not good and it also lacks the basic amenities like electricity, water, sanitation, etc. All these leads to health problems for the residents of this area.

Karol Bagh

Another busy market, which provides employment to a large number of children. A large number of children are self-employed as vendors, selling eatables, cold drinking water, cosmetics, handkerchief, etc. Rest of them are working in shops, tea stalls, dhabas, apprentices repairing cars, scooters and motorcycles. Another group of children are involved in rag picking and begging.

Besides these centrally located areas, there are other areas as well, where we can, find a high concentration of working and street children. Some of these areas are Motia Khan, Nehru Place, Naraina — Inderpuri, Azadpur, Vishwas Nagar, Shakoor Ki Dandi, Wazirpur, Jahangirpuri etc. In these areas too, the children are involved in varied activities. In some of these areas, basic facilities are not available. In Shakoor Ki Dandi, for example, which is a small scale industrial locality, the entire locality is divided in small narrow lanes surrounded with filth all around. The smell of chemicals makes one sick. The place where the little craftsmen work hardly has any ventilation and also lacks proper light. Their lives are totally dependent on the contractors, who earn profit by sucking their blood. They work for almost 18 hours a day thus losing their precious childhood. Sometimes they are not even paid a single penny inspite of working for so long hours.

Programmes for Working and Street Children: NGO Efforts[13]

The problem of child labour is a global phenomenon and it is a challenge for both the developed and developing countries. It is now an important social concern. Seeing at the magnitude of the problem, it can be said that the problem cannot be solved by a single person or a single agency. Hence there is a need to involve the NGOs in this endeavour. More than 200 NGOs throughout India are working in this direction. These NGOs are calling for the total abolition of child labour and child servitude.

So far as Delhi is concerned, here too, the NGOs are involved in this. More than a dozen NGOs are working with street and working children. The common features in their progammes are that they have health, and nutrition components, non-formal education, vocational training, recreational facilities and some also have counseling and saving schemes. But they vary from one another in their philosophies, approaches and strategies. The working of some of these NGOs are discussed in the succeeding pages.

Self Employed Women's Association (SEWA)

SEWA started work with rag-pickers in 1981 at East and West Nizamuddin, Minto Bridge, South Extension and Maharani Bagh. SEWA began with their non-formal education as most of the children were illiterate. SEWA also started job placement services, health and hygiene and saving scheme. The response was very good, so much so that they were at one time interacting with 2,000 children.

After working for some years with their own fund, they received funds from the Ministry of Labour, Government of India, to expand and strengthen their work. But in lieu of this fund, SEWA had to incorporate certain activities and implement programmes according to the dictates of the government. After the first instalment of funds, SEWA decided not to accept the second instalment. SEWA approached Plan International to fund their programmes. Once again SEWA was not happy with its decision to take financial help from the Plan International as they had to run their programmes to suit Plan International's objectives. In doing so, they were losing sight of their goals and objectives because earlier SEWA was having a good raport with the community, but once it started taking funds from Plan International, SEWA was doing nothing but just implementing programmes without the participation of the community. Thus, SEWA decided to go back to their earlier approach which is primarily involving community/group participation, once their Plan International Project comes to an end. Later on, SEWA extended the scope of its work in different areas which includes rag pickers at East and West Nizammuddin, Maharani Bagh, South Extension, R.K. Puram (Sector-I) and Turkman Gate.

Delhi Council for Child Welfare (DCCW)

DCCW, since late eighties, has been working with child ragpickers at Seemapuri. It started with around 80 children on the rolls, out of which 65 were regular and 25 of them were girls. If the children came to the center and remained there for two hours, they were paid an incentive of Rs. 2 per day. The main activities of the DCCW include — non-formal education, vocational training in weaving and a noon meal. Besides, there are facilities for bath and toilet too. According to DCCW, it was difficult to plan any new activity because children were not in regular numbers. They kept coming as and when they liked and many a times there were new faces. Due to all this, DCCW was not willing to carry on the activities and DCCW was ready to offer their premises to any NGO which was willing to work with street and working children or even take over the present activity.

Prayas

Prayas had its inception in 1988 as an emergency relief and rehabilitation measure for thousands of children rendered homeless due to a devastating fire in one of the slum areas in North Delhi at Jahangirpuri re-settlement colony. It started with 25 children and today it caters to the needs of 50,000 neglected, street and working children in the slum areas in Delhi, Gujarat and Bihar. It has worked in areas like Jahangirpuri, Azadpur, Vasant Vihar and Vasant Kunj slums in Delhi. Prayas works with a large number of urban-based child labourer through different projects in Delhi. Some of the occupations where children are working are auto-repair, workshops, garage, scavenging, rag picking, etc.

Prayas interventions focus on:

i) To reduce incidence of child labour by weaning them away from work and putting them into educational set ups through community awareness and their participation.
ii) To implement an integrated child centered programme through activities like, non-formal education, mid-day meal, clothes, recreation, health care services, counseling and skill development programmes along with its linking up and integration with the existing development programmes.
iii) Capacity building of the community for the long-term sustainability of the project.
iv) Developing a package for effective rehabilitation and socio-economic mainstreaming of child labour.

All these are provided through Prayas' 52 centres under thirteen different projects and three shelter homes.

Prayas also runs certain projects with the sole objective of elimination of child labour. Prayas street children's Project is one such project. This project is especially meant for rag-pickers and is being run in Jahangirpuri. It is a Drop-in-Centre which provides non-formal education, vocational training, food, clothes, recreation facilities, health care counseling, emotional support and rehabilitation for the care and development of street and working children.

Anupam Prayas Project, another such project, was started for children who come from families of traditional performing artists. At least 40 per cent of the working children are girls, mostly engaged in performing arts.

These communities also fall in the category of prostitution prone areas in certain authentic studies. But it is difficult to assess the extent of involvement of children in sex trade. Girl children in performing arts like folk dance are being used as objects of trade, alluring their clientele through their body movements which manifest in other sexual forms of exploitation.

In addition to these two projects, Prayas runs a 24-hour helpline called Childline (Telephone number 1098) for children in distress. Children and adults can report incidences of child labour and child abuse. Once the incidences are reported, child can get immediate shelter, food, medical aid and counseling.

Prayas is running a Prayas Bal Grih (PBG) at Hanuman Mandir, Connaught Place, since December 2002. It is meant for the runaway children especially those who have left their homes due to poverty, bad family conditions, alcoholic parents, etc. They belong to Bihar, Uttar Pradesh, Assam, West Bengal, Rajasthan and some areas of Delhi like Laxmi Nagar, Subhash Nagar and Patel Nagar. In case of Delhi, children leave their homes because their parents do not have time for them and also because they have step fathers and step mothers.

The (PBG) has thirty five children out of which twenty are working children. The target group is 6 to 18 years of age. It is being run by three members who look after these children. First of all, the workers try to restore the children i.e. to send them back to their homes. If they do not want to go back home, they are admitted to this center. Once they are admitted, the worker sees that the children are not involved in begging.

At this center, children are provided non-formal education from 10 a.m. to 1.00 p.m. on all days except Sundays. They are provided food and medical facilities. After studies, they watch T.V., play carom and luddo and in the night they have a Bal Sabha, where children discuss their problems, and their day to day schedule.

The twenty working children go out to work on Tuesdays and Saturdays and are involved in work such as making garlands, poories, getting the puja thali ready and also looking after shops. They deposit their money with the members of PBG and whenever they need money, the children can ask the members for money. They get a maximum of ten rupees at a time so that they don't indulge in bad habits.

Apart from all these centers, Prayas is running a Prayas Children's Home for Boys (PCHB) since 1997. Though the management of the Home is in the hands of Prayas, the Government of NCT of Delhi continues to provide funds. This Home is meant for the runaways, orphans, lost children and rag pickers. Top-most priority is given to restoration of children to the families. Only when the child is an orphan or family is untraceable or the child does not want to be restored, other alternatives like long stay homes and foster care are explored. The boys who come here are assigned to one of the eight sadans or houses, according to his age and background, to facilitate his stay, adjustment and activities. Besides, NFE, the children are given vocational training to infuse in them work habits, an attitude for honest living and team spirit. The activities in which they are involved are: book-binding, candle-making, chalk-stick making, cutting and tailoring, dyeing and tying, embroidery, jute work, knitting, etc.

Theatre Action Group (TAG)

TAG started working since January 16, 1988 with unlicenced coolie boys at the New Delhi Railway Station. As per the estimates of TAG, there were around 1,000 such boys at the railway station, but it was not easy to strike a rapport with them, as the boys were suspicious of adults. The boys used to gather at the community hall opposite the railway station, where they were served breakfast for which they were charged Rs. 2. Out of these two rupees, one rupee was saved on the boy's behalf. During the breakfast, the Hindi newspaper was read aloud to them and sometimes there were discussions on certain news items. In the evenings they were having formal literacy classes, recreation and discussions of their problems.

Prabhatara — Programme for Working Children

The programme was started in early nineties and the organization works with pavement dwellers residing near Bhikaji Cama Place and R.K. Puram. Most of the working children covered under this programme are migrants from Rajasthan. These children either pick rags or sell balloons, dusters and newspapers. None of the children covered under their programme had been to school but all of them were keen to study. Due to this keenness in studying and learning, Prabhatara started a literacy class in which twenty five to thirty children participated. Later on Prabhatara initiated health care and education programme as also a saving scheme.

Rag Pickers Project - Jahangirpuri

"Development, Justice and Peace" (DJP) is the development cell of the Catholic arch diocese of Delhi. They started their work in eighties in Jahangirpuri. The DJP had a large community health and adult education programme in this resettlement colony. On the demand of the children, an educational programme was started. About 200 children participated in the study classes. They paid Rs. 5 per month without the knowledge of their parents. The children were motivated to join open schools. Besides studies, the programme included recreational facilities, medical care and health education. Later on, a saving scheme was started, which became very popular with the children.

The working and functioning of all these NGOs shows that it is quite difficult and challenging to work with the working and street children. Most of the time the children were not coming in good numbers and were also not very regular. As such target numbers could not be fixed because the NGOs were working with a floating population.

An NGO Forum for street and working children was constituted in August 1987. The main function of this Forum was to work as an interest group for working and street children for initiating action in the area of child labour as also to share experiences and provide guidance to others. Secondly, the Forum was to promote cooperation and coordination amongst NGOs, individuals and government departments having programmes for working and street children. Thirdly, to create awareness about the issues which need to be addressed regarding working and street children, the possible interventions and the problems related to working in this area amongst government departments, NGOs and the public. Finally, the Forum publishes a quarterly newsletter on issues pertaining to street and working children.

South Asian Coalition on Child Servitude (SACCS)

Besides the above NGOs and the NGO Forum, there is the SACCS which in association with other NGOs is working on the issue of child labour in India. It designated 1995 as "Save the Childhood Year". This campaign called for the total abolition of child labour and child servitude and aimed at compulsory education for all children below 14 years of age and for the implementation of the UN Convention on the Rights of the Child. The NGOs participating in the campaign were to organize awareness campaigns in order to educate the public and pressurize the government to initiate rehabilitation programmes for the 55 million working children in India and to take action against their employers.

To launch save the Childhood Year 1995, a march was organized under the auspices of Bachpan Bachao Andolan (BBA) — Save the Childhood Movement. The march covered a distance of 150 Kms. through the main child labour areas of Delhi during January 19-25, 1995. The march was led by Kailash Satyarthi, Chairperson of SACCS. The marchers included hundreds of freed bonded children, child workers and social activists. The march began from the memorial of Mahatma Gandhi and then proceeded over to pass through the most prominent child labour pockets in Delhi, where over 60 public meetings, street dramas and cultural programmes were organized to share with the people the realities of child labour and gather support for save the Childhood Year.

The march concluded on January 25, 1995. It provided a good public forum for launching 1995 as Save the Childhood Year. Some of the freed bonded children graphically shared their experiences of work and sang parodies of life as child workers.

Salaam Balak Trust (SBT)

The SBT was started in 1986-87 at Paharganj under the chairpersonship of Mrs. Praveen Nair. The SBT has four contact points, four shelter homes and one community based programme. The four contact points are located at — (i) Hanuman Mandir, Connaught Place; (ii) GRP Police Thana, New Delhi Railway Station; (iii) New Delhi Railway Station Platform; and (iv) the Drop in Shelter, Basant Lane. The four shelter homes are i) Ashra, Paharganj; ii) Apna Ghar, Pahar Ganj Thana; iii) Arushi for girls at Uttam Nagar; and iv) Drop in Shelter, Basant Lane. The Drop in Shelter, Basant Lane is both a shelter home as well as contact point. The Community based programme, Akansha, is at the State Entry Road. Akansha provides education and vocational training to the working children.

The SBT's contact point at Hanuman Mandir, Connaught Place, was started in 1988. It looks after the run away children and provides education, shelter, nutrition and clothing to these children. The total number of children varies from 15-20. Presently they are having 17 children at the contact point. The target group is three to eighteen years. At this contact point, children are provided non-formal education, food and clothes. Most of the children at contact point are migrants (runaway) from Bihar, Uttar Pradesh, Madhya Pradesh and some from Rajasthan. These children left their homes as the environment their was not good. Hence, they come to Delhi in search of some job.

The center is being run by two members. These members provide non-formal education to the children on all days except Sunday, which is a holiday for the children. On Saturday's they have half day because these members have a meeting at the main branch of SBT, Paharganj. Some of the children of the contact point are working children. They are involved in works like making pooris, making garlands, and helping the shopkeepers. On Tuesdays and Saturdays, these children work at the mandir and earn somewhere between Rs. 80-200 on Tuesdays and Rs. 50-125 on Saturdays depending on the rush at the mandir. Besides, the money, they are provided food by their masters. Whatever money they earn, they deposit it to the members of the contact point. The children mostly spend the money on watching movies, buying transistors, video games, sometimes liquor, etc. The children are not allowed to do any addiction but if they do, they are punished for it.

Summing Up

On the whole it can be said that inspite of campaigns, newly introduced laws against child labour, exploitation of children continues. The problem of child labour in Delhi is no better. Child labour is spread throughout Delhi. The major cause of this problem is the migration from smaller towns to bigger cities. The vocations in which they are engaged are domestic help, shoe-shine boys, working at dhabas and tea-stalls, rag-picking, etc. These children are exposed to extreme weather conditions, traffic hazards, besides becoming victims of unhealthy habits like smoking, drinking, gambling etc. With the intervention of NGO's some of these problems are taken care of. A number of night shelters have come up where children can sleep at night. Besides, the NGOs are also providing non-formal education to the working children. The NGOs have taken up the right to primary education as a campaign issue. Most of them had started their campaigns from the child labour angle and later broadened it to free compulsory day time primary education as the most effective antidote against child labour. These NGOs have helped to build a basic infrastructure of educational, health and economic services for the child labourers.

REFERENCES

1. Mustafa, Mohd. and Sharma, Onkar, Child Labour in India — A Bitter Truth, Deep and Deep Publications, New Delhi, 1996, p. 6.
2. United Nations, Multilingual Demographic Dictionary, Population Studies No. 29, U.N. Department of Economic and Social Affairs, New York, 1958, pp. 22-23.
3. UNICEF: Exploitation of Working and Street Children, (E/ICEF/1986/CRP.3), March, 1986, pp. 14-15, (Unpublished).
4. Ibid., pp. 3-4.
5. Panicker, Rita and Nangia, Praveen, Working and Street Children of Delhi, National Labour Institute, Child Labour Cell, Noida, 1992, p. 4.
6. Census of India, 1991.
7. Main worker is one who has worked for major part of the year

preceding the date of enumeration, i.e., a person who was engaged in any economically productive activity for 183 days or six months or more during the year (usual status).

8. Marginal workers are those who worked any time at all in the year preceding the date of enumeration but did not work for major part of the year i.e., those who worked for less than 183 days or six months.
9. Website, mukti @ saccs. Unv. ernet. in.
10. Ibid.
11. Mustafa, Mohd. and Sharma, Onkar, op.cit., p. 2.
12. Panicker, Rita and Nangia, Praveen, op.cit., pp. 8-14.
13. Ibid., pp. 43-47.

6

Tiny Hands at Work

An Empirical Analysis

In the preceding chapter we have seen that child labour is spread throughout the NCT of Delhi. They are engaged in various vocations and face a lot of problem at the workplace. They are exposed to extreme weather conditions and the living conditions of working children are very unpleasant. Despite all these, their number is increasing day by day. In order to test and verify the facts relating to child labour in the NCT of Delhi, we conducted a survey in the different zones of NCT of Delhi. Accordingly, the present chapter focuses on the employment of child workers in the informal sector of Delhi and their socio-economic characteristics viz., occupation, income, education, housing and working conditions.

The analysis of the data is based on a survey of 250 child workers in the age group of 5 to 15 years. The child labourers were spread throughout the NCT of Delhi. For the present study we identified certain areas like Connaught Place, New Delhi Railway Station, Paharganj, Hanuman Mandir at Baba Kharag Singh Marg, Prachin Hanuman Mandir near Yamuna Bazaar, Chandni Chowk, Inter-State Bus Terminus, Yamuna Pushta, Naglamachi Jhuggi Pragati Maidan, Sarai Kale Khan, Lajpat Nagar, South Extension, Shadipur Depot and Mayur Vihar. In all the areas mentioned above, we served printed questionnaire to the child labourers in order to get their view points on the problem. The 250 child workers on whom the questionnaire was served belonged to vocations such as rag picking, shoe shining, mehandi applying, domestic help, washerman, barber, shoe-keeper, garland makers, poorie makers, hawkers, dhaba workers, road side café workers, glass beads roping, sequins work (salma-sitara embroidery) and cycle/scooter mechanic.

Age of the Child Workers

Our first query to them was regarding their age. Age is an important factor which shapes one's personality and enables one to determine the work responsibilities and occupation one wishes to join for economic independence. So far as the age of child workers is concerned, for our present study, we chose the children between the age group of 5-15 years. Table 6.1 shows the age-wise classification of child workers.

Table 6.1: Age Wise Classification of Child Workers

S.No.	*Age*	*No. of Respondents*	*Percentage*
1.	5-7	30	12
2.	8-10	60	24
3.	11-13	95	38
4.	14-15	65	26
	Total	**250**	**100**

From the above table it becomes clear that majority of them i.e. 95 (38%) child workers were in the age group of 11 to 13 years. In the second category were those children whose age group was 14 to 15 years and their number was 65 (26%). Followed by them, were the child workers in the age group of 8 to 10 years whose number was 60 (24%). The least number of child workers were 30 (12%) in the age group of 5 to 7 years. Thus, one can say that in Delhi, children at the age of 5 start working in some or the other vocation. This is the age when children of well to do families start going to school. But this is also the age when some children start working either due to poverty or broken family or lack of parental care or some other reason.

Native Place

After knowing their age, we moved on to the next query i.e. native place of child workers. Here we were surprised to note that the maximum number of child workers belonged to Bihar and Uttar Pradesh followed by Rajasthan, Madhya Pradesh, Orissa, West Bengal, Tamil Nadu, Assam and Delhi. Table 6.2 highlights the native place of child workers.

Table 6.2: Native Place of Child Workers

S.No.	*Native Place*	*No. of Respondents*	*Percentage*
1.	Bihar	88	35.2
2.	Uttar Pradesh	60	24
3.	Delhi	26	10.4
4.	Tamil Nadu	22	8.8
5.	Orissa	12	4.8
6.	Assam	12	4.8
7.	Madhya Pradesh	12	4.8
8.	West Bengal	10	4
9.	Rajasthan	08	3.2
	Total	**250**	**100**

The table reveals that the maximum number of child workers 88 (35.2%) were from Bihar followed by 60 (24%) from Uttar Pradesh. Our sample also comprised of sizeable number of child workers 26 (10.4%) from the NCT of Delhi. Children from as far as Tamil Nadu 22 (8.8%), Orissa 12 (4.8%), Assam 12 (4.8%), Madhya Pradesh 12 (4.8%) and West Bengal 10 (4%) have come to Delhi in search of work. The least number of child workers 08 (3.2%) were from Rajasthan. The data reveals the sorry state of affairs which is prevalent in most of the States especially Bihar and Uttar Pradesh from where families migrate and children runaway to Delhi in search of work.

Place of Stay

Another related query put to them was the place of stay. To this, they gave a long list of areas in which they were staying. The areas included Yamuna Pushta; Naglamachi Pragati Maidan Jhuggi; Jal Vihar Camp; Sarai Kale Khan; Nizamuddin; Laxmi Nagar; New Delhi Railway Station — Platforms and Patris; Shahdara; Seelampur; Salam Balak Trust's contact points at Hanuman Mandir, Baba Kharag Singh Marg, GRP Police Thana, New Delhi Railway Station and the drop in shelter at Basant Lane; and Prayas Bal Grih at Hanuman Mandir, Baba Kharag Singh Marg. For those children who were homeless and were runaways, the place of stay was their family, home and every thing. The child workers who were staying at the Platforms of New Delhi Railway Station considered the platform to be their homes and the various trains were their family and friends. Those children who were staying at the Salam Balak Trust contact point and Prayas Bal Grih treated it as their home, the workers as their parents and the other children staying there as their brothers, sisters and friends.

Gender

Our next query was related to gender. Out of the 250 respondents, 180 were male child workers and 70 were female child workers. The gender wise classification of child workers is given in Table 6.3.

Table 6.3: Gender Wise Classification of Child Workers

S.No.	*Gender*	*No. of Respondents*	*Percentage*
1.	Male	180	72
2.	Female	70	28
	Total	**250**	**100**

The above table indicates that in the NCT of Delhi there were 72 per cent (180) male child workers and the percentage of female child workers was 28 per cent (70). This difference in the percentage was due to the fat that the female child workers were not involved in all types of work which we chose for our study. They were mostly engaged as mehandi appliers, rag pickers, domestic workers, glass beads roping and sequins work (salma sitara embroidery). Most of the girls especially the ones engaged in sequins work, glass beads roping and rag picking, were staying with their parents and in all these activities, their mothers were also engaged. But in case of the female domestic workers, very few of them were staying with their parents.

Type of Family

Family plays a very important role in shaping the child's personality. Accordingly, we wanted to know from the child workers what type of a family they were having. To this, they gave a mixed response which is presented in Table 6.4. From the table one sees that 80 (32%) child workers belonged to nuclear families followed by 75 (30%) extended families. The least number of child workers 37 (14.8%) belonged to joint family. Another set of 58 (23.2%) children belonged to single parent family where either the father or mother had died or they were not staying together.

Though the child workers explained the kind of family they belonged, but most of them were reluctant to answer this query, as they were runaways and were not having contact with their families. However, on our insistence they replied our query and further added that their workplace was their family.

Table 6.4: Type of Family to Which Child Labourers Belonged

S.No.	*Type of family*	*No. of Respondents*	*Percentage*
1.	Joint	37	14.8
2.	Nuclear	80	32
3.	Extended	75	30
4.	Single Parent	58	23.2
	Total	**250**	**100**

Number of Family Members

Another related query was regarding the number of family members. Table 6.5 gives the number of family members in a child workers family.

Table 6.5: Number of Members in Child Workers Family

S.No.	*No. of Family Members*	*No. of Respondents*	*Percentage*
1.	1-4	27	10.8
2.	4-8	125	50
3.	8-12	98	39.2
	Total	**250**	**100**

The table reveals that 125 (50%) child workers belonged to such families where there were 4 to 8 members. Similarly 98 (39.2%) child workers belonged to families which had 8 to 12 members. Only 27 (10.8%) workers belonged to families which had 1 to 4 members. Thus, one can say that in a family which had more than 6 members, it is difficult for one person to run the house. Hence there is no other alternative but to send the child to work rather than to school in order to supplement family income. The children who belonged to the small family category i.e. 1 to 4 members, worked either because there was no earning member in the family or their parents were alcoholic. Most of the children of this category added that they had to work because their father had died and being the eldest child, it was their duty to look after the family. Some other workers opined that their father were addicts and used to beat their mothers after consuming liquor. As such, the children had no other alternative, but to work. Thus, we see that whether the child belonged to small or large family, they are forced to work for some reason or the other.

Number of Brothers and Sisters

Still another related query was regarding the number of brothers and sisters, the workers had. To this, again we had multiple responses. The child workers had a maximum of eight brothers and sisters and a minimum of two.

Engagement of the Brothers and Sisters

Our next query was regarding the engagement of the worker's brothers and sisters in one occupation or the other. An answer to this query can be found in Table 6.6.

Table 6.6: Brothers and Sisters Engaged in Job

S.No.	*Engaged in Job*	*No.of Respondents*	*Percentage*
1.	Yes	138	55.2
2.	No	112	44.8
	Total	**250**	**100**

It becomes clear from the table that 138 (55.2%) child workers brothers and sisters were engaged in some occupation or the other. Whereas in case of 112 (44.8%) child workers, they were not engaged in any occupation. Those children whose brothers and sisters were engaged in occupation opined that they belonged to large families and had to work because of parents pressure and also in order to supplement family income.

Related to this query was the engagement of brothers and sisters in rag-picking work. Table 6.7 makes clear that only 58 (23.2%) of workers brothers and sisters were engaged in rag-picking work. Whereas 192 (76.8%) workers gave a negative reply. In case of rag picking work, it was found that the brothers and sisters of those workers were engaged in rag picking who themselves were rag pickers. In most of the cases, it was the female rag pickers whose younger siblings were engaged in rag picking. It was like a team work where the mother led the team and the daughters were the members of the team. We met around six girls who were having four sisters each, and all engaged in rag picking work. These girls were from Tamil Nadu and Assam and were operating in Lajpat Nagar Market and South Extension. These female rag pickers revealed that once they attain the age of 12-13, they stop rag picking work and start working as domestic help in the nearby areas. In case of male rag pickers too, we found some of the siblings engaged in this work. But their number was very few.

Table 6.7: Brothers and Sisters Engaged in Rag Picking

S.No.	*Engaged in Rag Picking*	*No. of Respondents*	*Percentage*
1.	Yes	58	23.2
2.	No	192	76.8
	Total	**250**	**100**

We further asked them how much the workers younger siblings earned out of rag picking. To this, they replied that their earning was somewhere between Rs. 200-Rs. 300, per week, depending upon the amount of labour they were putting.

Residential Accommodation

From the family members, we moved on to the residential accommodation of the child workers family. In this category, our first query to the child workers was that where does their family live? The answer to this query is given in Table 6.8.

Table 6.8: Residential Accommodation of the Child Workers Family

S. No.	*Type of House*	*No. of Respondents*	*Percentage*
1.	Own House	84	33.6
2.	Rented House	72	28.8
3.	Jhuggi Jhopari	94	37.6
	Total	**250**	**100**

The table revealed that 94 (37.6%) child workers family lived in 'jhuggi jhopari,' 84 (33.6%) in their own house and 72 (28.8%)

in rented house. The families which were living in 'jhuggi jhopari' were mostly those who had migrated from Bihar, Uttar Pradesh and Tamil Nadu, to Delhi, in search of job.

Our next query was regarding space in the house. Table 6:9 reveals the living condition of workers family i.e. the space in their house.

Table 6.9: Space in the House

S.No.	*Space in their house*	*No. of Respondents*	*Percentage*
1.	One room including kitchen	110	44
2.	One room plus kitchen	58	23.2
3.	Two rooms plus kitchen	82	32.8
	Total	**250**	**100**

The table highlights that 110 (44%) of the families were living in one room including kitchen. In this category the jhuggi jhopari families have also been included. About 82 (32.8%) families were living in a house which had two rooms and a kitchen. Whereas 58 (23.2%) families were having one room plus kitchen. These figures revealed that the families were not better off and had to compromise with the living condition. In one small or two rooms, around 10 to 12 people were living.

Profession of Parents

Another related query was regarding the profession of parents i.e. both father and mother. We could not get a very clear response to this query hence the tabular analysis is not being presented here. However, on the basis of the data which we had collected, one can say that the parents were in those profession which could hardly provide two square meal to the family. The child workers family who were staying in Bihar and Uttar Pradesh were mostly working on the fields. Here they added that both the parents were working on the fields. Those families who had migrated to Delhi from Bihar and Uttar Pradesh and were staying in jhuggies, the ladies of these families were mostly engaged in glass beads roping, sequins work and some also in tailoring. So far as the male members are concerned, they were found engaged in auto driving, working in laundries, selling fruits and vegetables, working in factories and also as security guards.

The ladies of those families who had migrated from Tamil Nadu, were engaged in rag picking and domestic help. Their husbands were mostly drunkards earning no money. They used to stay at home creating nuisance for the whole family.

Thus, we see that the profession of child workers parents range from auto driving, working on fields, working in laundries, selling fruits and vegetables to domestic help and rag picking.

Addiction

From profession of parents, we moved on to the addiction of guardian. Our query to the child workers was whether their parents were having any addiction. The answer to this query is presented in Table 6.10.

Table 6.10: Addiction of Guardian

S.No.	*Type of Addiction*	*No. of Respondents*	*Percentage*
1.	Drinking	122	48.8
2.	Smoking	66	26.4
3.	Tabacco Chewing	34	13.6
4.	None	28	11.2
	Total	**250**	**100**

The table reveals that 122 (48.8%) child workers guardian were having the addiction of drinking where as 66 (26.4%) were addicted to smoking. In our questionnaire we had given the next option — drugs. But we were surprised that none of the parents were taking drugs. Besides drinking and smoking, they were addicted to tobacco chewing. The above data reveals that 34 (13.6%) were addicted to tobacco chewing. We were further surprised to note that 28 (11.2%) were not having any type of addiction. This is a good sign in the sense that if you are not addicted to anything then chances are there that you can stop your child from any type of addiction. If the guardians themselves are addicts then there are chances that the children can also become addicts. They have a tendency and inquisitiveness to learn what their elders are doing. This is clearly reflected from our next table. Here we would like to add that not only the males, some of the females were also having addiction. Some of them were addicted to tobacco chewing and some even to smoking bidi. These undesirable habits found among the members in the family of child workers drives most of the children to take work.

Besides the guardians, we were also curious to know whether the child workers themselves were addicts. When we put this query, we were surprised to note that out of 250 child workers, 198 were having addiction of some type or the other. Table 6.11 describes the type of addiction, the child workers were having.

Table 6.11: Nature of Addiction of Child Workers

S.No.	Type of Addiction	No. of Respondents	Percentage
1.	Drinking	90	36
2.	Chewing gutka	33	13.2
3.	Smoking Charas/Ganja/Bidi	75	30
4.	None	52	20.8
	Total	250	100

From the table it becomes clear that 90 (36%) of them were addicted to drinking, 75 (30%) to smoking charas/ganja/bidi and 33 (13.2%) to chewing gutka. Only 52 (20.8%) of them were not having addiction of any kind. The reason behind this is that out of 52 child workers, most of them were staying with their parents and were those whose family condition was somewhat better. There were a number of boys who frankly admitted that they take country liquor almost every day. One boy aged 10, selling locks/keys and chains at the New Delhi Railway Station, admitted with lots of smile on his face that he spends Rs. 15-20 on gutka every day. Another boy of the same age group, who was working at a roadside café in Lajpat Nagar, also admitted that he was addicted to gutka chewing and he spends around Rs. 300 per month on this. These instances are of those boys who took to addiction on their own. But there were another set of child workers who were forced to consume liquor and charas/ganja.There were a group of boys at the Hanuman Mandir, Baba Kharag Singh Marg, who complained that they were forced to take charas and ganja by some senior boys in whose company they live.

When we asked them since how long they are addicts, they replied that once they get a job and start getting money, they get addicted to one thing or the other. There were boys who were addicts since last five or six years. But there were also some new boys who were getting into this habit. On the basis of all these, one can say that there are certain factors due to which a child worker becomes an addict. It can be the family environment, the surrounding in which they work and live, the compulsion, as we have seen, and sometimes curiosity to taste something new.

Factors Responsible for Child Labour

We all know that child labour is not a new problem and a number of factors are responsible for the emergence of child labour in the NCT of Delhi. Accordingly, our next query was regarding factors which led them to work as a child labour. We got a mixed response for this query (Table 6.12).

Table 6.12: Factors that Led them to Work

S.No.	*Factors Responsible*	*No. of Respondents*	*Percentage*
1.	Broken Family	45	18
2.	Alcoholic Parents	32	12.8
3.	Lack of Parental Care	20	8
4.	Low Interest in Studies	33	13.2
5.	Pressure from Parents	46	18.4
6.	Illiteracy among Parents	10	4
7.	To supplement Family Income	36	14.4
8.	For Better Living	28	11.2
	Total	**250**	**100**

On the basis of this table, one can say that the most important factor which led them to work was pressure from parents. About 46 (18.4%) children started working only because their parents wanted them to work. This is due to the illiteracy and ignorance of parents. They only think about the present condition which is their only concern and worry. They never think of their future. They are fully satisfied with the present earning of their children. As such children start working. Most of these boys were those who were interested in studying at least upto some level but had to give up because their parents were not ready. Another related and major factor was broken family. Around 45 (18%) of them started working because of broken family. They pointed out that their parents used to fight and were later separated and got married to someone else. Some of them were having step mothers and some had step fathers. Due to all this, they got irritated and started working.

Yet another related factor was to supplement family income. The child workers (36) said that they joined work because they had no other option. Since their families were large and one or two persons income was not sufficient for the entire family. Thus they joined work so that they can provide extra income to the family.

Around 33 (13.2%) child workers reported that they had low interest in studies and did not want to study further. This aversion has been created because of their family circumstances. Majority do not have a good family environment. To study one needs a calm and peaceful environment. Since this was lacking in most families of child workers they lose their interest in studies and as such they all became child workers. They further added that if they work instead of studying they can earn something for the family as well as for themselves. Another set of child workers (32) said that their father was alcoholic and did not take care of his family. After drinking they used to either beat their wives or children and sometimes the family had nothing to eat. Due to such family conditions the children had no option but to work.

Another reason which led the child workers to work was to have a better living standard. Around 28 (11.2) child workers were of the view that the conditions in which they and their family lived was not good. They were not having sufficient space to live, sufficient food to eat, enough clothes to cover themselves and money to meet their other demands like medical care, education etc. Because of all these they got frustrated and thought of joining work so that they can have a better living standard.

Still another factor was lack of parental care. There were 20 (8%) working children who opined that they never received any love and affection from their parents. There were many reasons for this. For example, step parents, poverty, bad habits among the parents and lack of time. In some cases there was very strict discipline for the child and no discipline for the parents which acted as a forerunner of delinquency. All these led to neglect of children on the parts of parents. Being deprived of love and affection and a congenial atmosphere at home, they ran away from their homes and started working. Though the money which they earned, did not provide parental love and affection, but they were satisfied that they were living a life of their own without any interference.

Finally, the illiteracy among parents also led the child workers to work. We came across 10 (4%) such children who were working because their parents were illiterate. They were not knowing the importance of education and thought that if children start working instead of going to school, they can earn more as there will be more helping hand. Keeping this point in view, they made their children work. Besides, poverty also compels some of the parents to send their children to seek employment.

Apart from all these, there are certain other factors responsible for the emergence of child labour in the informal sector of the NCT of Delhi. Some of these factors are lack of employment opportunities, lack of physical and mental fitness due to malnutrition, sheer encouragement to take up jobs instead of going to school, poverty, and lack of protective labour legislation. All these factors have contributed to the problem of child labour.

Education

Education plays an important role in one's life in the sense that it helps in shaping the right kind of life style in the human beings. It is education which turns children into a social and human being. Education formal or informal aims at developing the positive quality of the child and helps the individual realise his potentialities. Accordingly, the child workers were asked to state their educational qualification/background. Table 6.13 shows the educational status of the working children.

Table 6.13: Educational Qualification of Child Workers

S.No.	*Educational Qualification*	*No. of Respondents*	*Percentage*
1.	Primary	138	55.2
2.	Secondary	34	13.6
3.	Uneducated	78	31.2
	Total	**250**	**100**

It is evident from the above table that out of 250 working children, 138 (55.2%) of them had education upto primary level, 34 (13.6%) upto middle level and 78 (31.2%) were uneducated. The reasons for their not being educated and not completing their studies have already been discussed in preceding pages.

After knowing their educational qualification, we wanted to

know whether they were drop outs. Table 6.14 shows the drop out rate of the child workers.

Table 6.14: Whether the Child was a Drop Out?

S.No.	*Whether a Drop Out?*	*No. of Respondents*	*Percentage*
1.	Yes	172	68.8
2.	No	78	31.2
	Total	**250**	**100**

It is disheartening to note that out of 250 working children, 162 (68.8%) were dropouts. Of this, maximum number of them became a drop out after primary education and some after middle education i.e. they could not complete their secondary education. There were 78 (31.2%) child workers who were not drop outs. All the 78 child workers were uneducated. Thus we see that out of 250 working children, not even a single child had completed his education upto the secondary level. In order to stop this drop out rate there is a need to provide vocational education to all the working children after they complete their primary education.

After knowing the drop out rate, we asked them to assign reasons for being drop out. Table 6.15 shows the various reasons assigned for being a drop out.

Table 6.15: Reasons for Being a Drop Out

S.No.	*Reasons for being drop out*	*No. of Respondents*	*Percentage*
1.	Family Condition	80	46.5
2.	Lack of School Facilities	26	15.1
3.	Motive of earning for the family	20	11.6
4.	Motive to get pocket money for personal use	22	12.8
5.	Under the influence of friends	24	14.0
6.	Were not drop outs	78	31.2
	Total	**250**	**100**

On the basis of above table we can say that there are a number of reasons assigned for being drop out. The foremost reason is the family condition i.e. large families with one or two working members. The table reveals that 80 (46.5%) child workers had to leave their studies in between because their family condition did not permit them to continue their studies. Secondly, it can be seen that in 26 (15.1 %) cases, there was lack of school facilities i.e. either there were no schools after primary level or they were very far from the residence of child labourers. Due to this, the children could not continue their studies. Another reason for being a drop out was that 24 (14 %) child workers started working under the influence of friends. They opined that their friends had lured them to stop their studies and join them in work as it would bring them lots of money. Without knowing the consequences, the child workers, stopped their studies and started working under the influence of their friends. Around 22 (12.8 %) of them left their studies only with the motive of earning some pocket money for themselves. Since their families were not giving them any pocket money, they thought if they start working, they can earn some pocket money for themselves. Only 20 (11.6 %) child workers left studies with a motive to earn for the family. These 20 working children opined that they were working with the sole objective of earning for the family and providing them a better living standard. The rest of the child workers 78 (31.2%) were not drop outs as they were uneducated. Hence they did not assign any reason for being drop outs.

Work and Education

Another education related query put to the child workers was whether work is more important than education. The table (6.16) given below shows the attitude of child workers towards work and education.

Table 6.16: Importance Given to Work Rather than Education

S.No.	*Importance Given to Work*	*No. of Respondents*	*Percentage*
1.	Yes	208	83.2
2.	No	42	16.8
	Total	**250**	**100**

It was disheartening to note that 208 (83.2%) child workers gave importance to work rather than education and only 42 (16.8%) wanted to study. It is clear from the table that majority of the child workers preferred to work rather than study. Even those who had given importance to education, wanted to continue their work and study side by side.

Importance Given to Work

After knowing their attitude towards work and education, we asked them why they gave importance to work. To this we got a mixed response which is presented in Table 6.17.

Table 6.17: Reasons for Giving Importance to Work

S.No.	*Reasons*	*No. of Respondents*	*Percentage*
1.	To earn money	50	20
2.	Not interested in studies	38	15.2
3.	No earning member in the family	12	4.8
4.	To supplement family income	28	1.2
5.	Family environment	62	24.8
6.	To learn the work	17	6.8
7.	Compulsion from Parents	43	17.2
	Total	**250**	**100**

The above table indicates that 62 (24.8%) child workers gave importance to work because of family environment, 50 (20%) said they wanted to earn money and 43 (17.2%) opined that it was due to parents' compulsion. Besides these, 38 (15.2%) were not interested in studies, 28 (11.2%) wanted to supplement family income, 17 (6.8%) wanted to learn the work and 12 (4.8%) had no earning member in the family. Thus, we see that a number of reasons have been given to prove that work is more important than education. It is clear from the table that majority of the child workers preferred to work not only because of poor economic condition of the family or because they want to earn money, but also because neither the parents nor the children themselves were interested in school education. Both the parents as well as the child workers viewed life from the point of view of present small return without education, rather than future higher (probably) returns after a certain level of education.

Interest in Studies

Based on the above query, the child workers were asked to state their interest in studying. The table below (6.18) shows the child workers interest in studies.

Table 6.18: Classification of Child Workers According to their Interest in Studies

S.No.	*Interest in Studies*	*No. of Respondents*	*Percentage*
1.	Full time	25	10
2.	Non formal Education	145	58
3.	Not at all	80	32
	Total	**250**	**100**

The above table shows that 80 (32%) child workers were not interested in studies. 145 (58%) of them were interested in attending non formal education and only 25 (10%) were interested in full time education. During the course of our survey we observed that children at Yamuna Pushta, New Delhi Railway Station, Paharganj and Hanuman Mandir, Baba Kharag Singh Marg, besides engaged in various vocations, were also getting non formal education at the various contact points of Salam Balak Trust and Prayas.

Occupation of the Child Workers

From education, we moved to occupation of the child workers. Children in the NCT of Delhi pick up any work that is near to their place. Their parents and friends were the main motivators for them to undertake certain types of work. Table 6.19 presents the various occupation of the children in which they were involved.

Table 6.19: Classification of Child Workers on the Basis of Type of Work

S.No.	*Type of Work*	*No. of Respondents*	*Percentage*
1.	Rag Picking	60	24
2.	Cycle/Scooter Mechanic	22	8.8
3.	Dhaba/Road side Café	35	14
4.	Shoe shining	8	3.2
5.	Hawkers	28	11.2
6.	Washermen	6	2.4
7.	Barbers	5	2
8.	Mehandi Appliers	12	4.8
9.	Glass Beads Roping	15	6
10.	Domestic Help	20	8
11.	Sequins Work (Salma Sitara Embroidery)	15	6
12.	Garland Making	10	4
13.	Shoe keepers	6	2.4
14.	Poorie Making	8	3.2
	Total	**250**	**100**

The above table indicates that fourteen categories of work are being undertaken by children in the informal sector of NCT of Delhi. Of these fourteen categories, girls were engaged only in six or seven types of work. These works are domestic help, mehandi applying, glass beads roping, sequins work, garland making, rag picking and shoe keeping to some extent. But so far as boys are concerned, they are engaged in all types of work except sequins work. The table shows that majority 60 (24%) of the child workers were engaged in rag picking followed by dhaba workers/road side café 35 (14%). At number three were hawkers 28 (11.2%) followed by cycle/scooter mechanic 22 (8.8%) and domestic help 20 (8%). 15 each (6%) were engaged in glass beads roping and sequins work (salma sitara embroidery). Besides these, there were 12 (4.8%) children who were engaged in mehandi applying, 10 (4%) in garland making, 8 (3.2%) in poorie making, 6 each (2.4%) in washing and shoe keeping and 5 (2%) in hair cutting work. Thus we see that children are engaged in all types of work no matter what their age is.

Mode of Payment

After classifying them on the basis of the type of work they are doing, we asked them about the mode of payment. The table below (6.20) shows the mode of payment of the child workers engaged in various type of work.

Table 6.20: Children's Classification According to the Mode of Payment

S.No.	Mode of Payment	No. of Respondents	Percentage
1.	Daily Wage	50	20
2.	Weekly Payment	32	12.8
3.	Monthly Salary	168	67.2
	Total	**250**	**100**

The above table indicates that 168 (67.2%) of the child workers got monthly salary followed by daily wage to 50 (20%) child workers and weekly payment to 32 (12.8%). The daily wage workers mostly included those engaged in shoe-keeping, garland making, poorie making, hawkers who were engaged by themselves, shoe-shining, mehandi applying etc. Those getting weekly payment included rag pickers (some of them), cycle/ scooter mechanics, glass beads roping and sequins work. Sometimes the children engaged in glass beads roping and sequins work got fortnightly payment. In the third category were those children who got monthly salary. These children were engaged as domestic help, washermen, barbers, dhaba/road side café, and some of the hawkers.

Wages

Wages determine the economic status of a household. The wages which the working children receive depends upon various factors like, nature of job-skilled, semi-skilled or unskilled; duration of working hours; risk involved in the work; nature of employment — daily wage, contract or regular; etc. The following table (6.21) indicates the income of child workers in the NCT of Delhi.

Table 6.21: Monthly Income of Child Workers

S.No.	*Monthly Income*	*No. of Respondents*	*Percentage*
1.	300-500	80	32
2.	500-700	66	26.4
3.	700-1,000	74	29.6
4.	Above 1,000	30	12
	Total	**250**	**100**

The table indicates that majority of working children 80 (32%) received a monthly income between Rs. 300 to Rs. 500. The wages of working children in Delhi ranges from Rs. 300 to Rs. 1,500 per month. There were 66 (26.4%) children who earned between Rs. 500 to Rs. 700 per month followed by 74 (29.6%) children whose earnings were between Rs. 700 to Rs. 1,000. Besides, there were 30 (12%) such children who earned more than Rs. 1,000 per month. All the children received their income in cash, some on daily basis, some weekly and some monthly depending upon the type of work they were doing.

Share of Wages Given to Family

Our next query to them was regarding their share to their families income. The response to this query was mixed and hence it is not being presented in tabular form. On the basis of our survey we can say that almost half of them (125) were contributing in the ratio of 50:50 i.e. they were keeping 50 per cent with them and were giving 50 per cent to their families. Here one thing which was very strange was that though most of them were runaways, they were contributing to their families. However, there were also those who were not contributing a single penny to their families. Their main grievance was that they were thrown out of their homes and as such were not in touch with them. Another set of child workers opined that they do not send money on a monthly basis. They used to save some amount every month and after saving a handsome amount, say somewhere between Rs. 1,000 to Rs. 2,000, they send that amount to their families. Yet another set of working children used to contribute to their families only on special occasions for example, wedding in the family, when someone fell ill or on festivals. One strange case we found was that of a young boy who was contributing to his family in a very unique way i.e some amount to his parents and some to his grand parents. Finally, there were some other boys who kept a very small amount with them and gave the rest amount to their parents. They were the ones who were staying with their parents.

Wages Spent on Themselves

Another similar query put to them was how much they were spending on themselves. Here again we got a similar response as the above query, so a tabular presentation is not given. Some were spending 50 per cent of the salary, some 100 per cent, some only 20 per cent and the rest between 30 to 60 per cent. They used to spend their income on movies, liquor, ganja, charas, gutka, sometimes clothes and even food.

Area of Operation

After getting the details of their income and spending, we asked them in which place/area they were working. Once again we got a mixed response and we could not present a tabular analysis of the data. Their place/area of work was scattered and included New Delhi Railway Station, Paharganj, Hanuman Mandir, Prachin Hanuman Mandir, ISBT, Chandni Chowk, Darya Ganj, Yamuna

Pushta, Naglamachi Pragati Maidan Jhuggi, Sarai Kale Khan, Lajpat Nagar, South Extension, Shadipur Depot and Mayur Vihar.

Distance

After classifying the areas in which they were working, we asked them how far was the distance between the place of work and their residence. The table (6.22) below shows the distance between the child workers residence and the place of work.

Table 6.22: Distance between the Place of Work and Child Workers Residence

S.No.	Distance	No. of Respondents	Percentage
1.	Very Near	137	54.8
2.	Short Distance	66	26.4
3.	Long Distance	47	18.8
	Total	**250**	**100**

The table reveals that 137 (54.8%) child workers were staying very near to their work place. They were the ones who were staying at New Delhi Railway Station, Hanuman Mandir, Yamuna Pushta, Naglamachi Pragati Maidan Jhuggi and were involved in work in and around their residence. Another group of child workers 66 (26.4), were staying at a short distance from their work place. They were the ones who were staying at Jal Vihar Camp, Sarai Kale Khan and Pahar Ganj and working in the areas like Lajpat Nagar, South Extension, New Delhi Railway Station and Hanuman Mandir. There were 47 (18.8)%) child workers who had to cover a long distance to reach their work place for example, the washermen were staying at Pahar Ganj and were working at Yamuna Pushta. There were some other boys who were staying at Karol Bagh and were working at Shadipur Depot. Still some other workers were staying at Sarai Kale Khan and Nizammudin and were working at South Extension. Thus we see that the young children had to travel long distance in order to earn something for themselves and their family.

Age at the Time of Joining Work

The children enter work life at an early age because most of them are school drop outs and they have no other alternative, but to join a gainful employment. The following table (6.23) shows the age at which the children started working.

Table 6.23: Age at Which the Child Workers Started Working

S.No.	*Age*	*No. of Respondents*	*Percentage*
1.	5-7	103	41.2
2.	8-10	92	36.8
3.	10-12	55	22.0
	Total	**250**	**100**

The above table indicates that 103 (41.2%) child workers entered workforce between the age of 5 to 7 years. 92 (36.8%) of them started working between the age of 8-10 years and the least number of children 55 (22%), started their work at a bit later stage i.e. between the age of 10-12. Thus, we see that there is no age at which the children start working. Though in the Constitution it is stated that children should not be allowed to work till they attain the age of 14, yet they are being employed as early as 5 years.

Our next query to them was whether this was their first job and if yes, what was the working condition? Table 6.24 shows that whether this was their first job.

Table 6.24: Whether this was the First Job of the Child Workers?

S.No.	*Whether this was their first job?*	*No. of Respondents*	*Percentage*
1.	Yes	187	74.8
2.	No	63	25.2
	Total	**250**	**100**

The table reveals that it was the first job for 187 (74.8%) children. For 63 (25.2%) children it was not their first job. Those who said that it was not their first job, had changed their jobs twice or thrice in a span of two-three years. There were two boys who had run away from their homes in Bihar and came to Delhi in search of work. Initially they worked at dhaba near the New Delhi Railway Station for three months. They left this work as it was not of their liking. Then they joined a tea-stall where they worked for next two months. Here also they could not adjust. Finally, they went to a shop in Paharganj where small boys were working as cycle/scooter mechanic. They liked the place and work and finally decided to stick to that work. Since then (last two years) they are working as scooter mechanic. Similarly, there were some other children who initially were rag pickers but later switched over to domestic help.

In case of those children, who were still in their first job, we observed that the dhaba workers started their work at the dhaba and they were still working there. But there was a peculiar thing about these dhaba workers that after working at one dhaba for sometime, they switched over to some other dhaba and then to the next. We observed that they work at one dhaba for six months or so and then move to the next. In case of rag pickers, it was their first job. They started with rag picking and continue to pick rag. Some of the hawkers changed their work in the sense that initially they were selling something else and later were selling some other item because they were not getting much profit. Though they changed the items as per their requirement, yet they were in the same work i.e. hawking. Thus, in their case too, as in the case of dhaba workers, their job was treated as first job. On the whole one can say that once the child worker was engaged in one work, he/she continued to be in that very work. Only if the work was not suitable and the working condition was not good, they changed their work.

Working Condition

So far as the working condition is concerned, all the 187 (74.8%) child workers said that it was alright but there were certain things which were lacking at the workplace. Some said there were no toilet facility, some complained about drinking water, others said they have to work in open space, etc. Sometimes the child workers were abused, sometimes beaten up and sometimes even their salaries were cut. On the whole, leaving aside the above problems, the working condition was normal.

Duration of Present Job

After knowing the working condition of the child workers, we wanted to know since how long they are in the present job. Table 6.25 shows the duration of the present job.

Table 6.25: Duration of the Present Job

S.No.	Duration	No. of Respondents	Percentage
1.	6 months — 2 years	88	35.2
2.	2 years — 3 years	56	22.4
3.	3 years and more	106	42.4
	Total	**250**	**100**

From the above table it becomes clear that 106 (42.4%) child workers were in the present job since last three years and more, followed by 88 (35.2%) of them since six months to two years. The least number of them 56 (22.4%), were in the present job since two-three years. The first category of child workers, i.e., 106, were those children who were engaged in rag picking, sequins work, glass beads roping, mehandi applying, dhaba workers, etc. Thus, it can be said that there are certain vocations in which children continue to work for a longer period.

Working Hours

As per the law, children should not work for longer hours. But in practice the law is not strictly followed. When we asked them about their daily working hours, they gave a number of mixed response which is presented in Table 6.26.

Table 6.26: Daily Working Hours of the Child Workers

S.No.	Working Hours	No. of Respondents	Percentage
1.	8-10	32	12.8
2.	10-12	82	32.8
3.	12-14	93	37.2
4.	14-16	43	17.2
	Total	**250**	**100**

The above table indicates that irrespective of occupation majority of child workers 93 (37.2%) were found to work for 12 to 14 hours a day. We were surprised to note that none of the children had normal working hours of less than four hours a day. More than 14-16 hours of work were undertaken by 43 (17.2%) child workers. There were 82 (32.8%) children who were working for 10-12 hours a day. Only 32 (12.8%) children used to work for 8-10 hours a day. Those children who were self-employed i.e. working on their own, were in an advantageous position in the sense that their working hours were flexible. Whenever they wanted to earn more money, they used to work for a longer time. Children falling in this category were rag pickers, mehandi appliers, some of the hawkers, shoe keepers and garland makers. On the other hand, those children who were employed by some other person were the sufferers in the sense that their working hours were neither fixed nor flexible. Even if they worked for longer hours, they were not paid extra for that work.

Hours Spent Outside House

After knowing the working hours of the child labourers, we asked them how many hours they spent outside their house. The following table (6.27) indicates the hours which the children spend outside their homes.

Table 6.27: Time Spent by Child Workers Outside their Home

S.No.	*Hours spent Outside Home*	*No. of Respondents*	*Percentage*
1.	8-12	56	22.4
2.	12-16	102	40.8
3.	16-20	92	36.8
	Total	**250**	**100**

The table reveals that a large number of working children 102 (40.8%) remained outside their homes for more than 12 to 16 hours. Another 92 (36.8%) of them remained outside their homes even for a more longer period i.e 16 to 20 hours. Only 56 (22.4%) child workers were spending 8 to 12 hours outside their homes. Since most of the workers were runaway and not having any home they were spending maximum time outside their home.

Activities During Spare Time

Every human being needs some spare time to do things of his liking. One tries to relax during the spare time and for this one undertake's certain activities like watching movies, playing, talking with friends etc. Accordingly, we asked the child workers what they do during their spare time. The following table (6.28) shows what the children do during their spare time.

Table 6.28: Activities which the Children do During their Spare Time

S.No.	Activities	No. of Respondents	Percentage
1.	Play	34	13.6
2.	Rest	25	10
3.	Watch Movie	146	58.4
4.	Study	22	8.8
5.	Do some other work	23	9.2
	Total	**250**	**100**

The child workers get very less spare time. But whatever spare time they get, they try to utilise it in the best possible manner. The table reveals that a majority of the child workers 146 (58.4%), watched movies during their spare time. Others 34 (13.6%) played carrom, ludo or cricket. There were 25 (10%) children who preferred to take rest as they thought, they had very less time to relax. Another 23 (9.2%) of them did some other work like going to temple, talking to their friends, going to India Gate and having fun in water at the India Gate lawns. A very small number of children 22 (8.8%) preferred to study. Since they were drop outs and were willing to study, they thought of utilizing their spare time in studying.

Rest Interval

After getting information on what they do during spare time, we asked them whether they got any rest interval other than lunch break. The answer to this query is given in Table 6.29.

Table 6.29: Whether the Working Children were Getting any Rest Interval Other than Lunch Break?

S.No.	Whether they got rest interval?	No. of Respondents	Percentage
1.	Yes	48	19.2
2.	No	202	80.8
	Total	**250**	

It was disheartening to note that a large number of children 202 (80.8), were not getting any rest interval during the course of the day. Only 48 (19.2%) working children replied that they were getting a kind of rest interval. These children were mostly those who were working at dhabas. After the rush hour (lunch time), the worker got half an hour or so to relax. After relaxing, they again went to work as it was time for serving evening tea and snacks. The rag pickers at the New Delhi Railway Station opined that they were not having any rest intervals as such because the trains were coming and going on one platform or the other and they had to rush in order to collect the left over from the trains.

Weekly Holidays

Weekly holidays are a must in order to relax and refresh oneself. Whether it is a child or an elderly person, every one needs the weekly holidays. In this background, we wanted to know from the child workers whether they were getting any weekly holidays. The following table (6.30) shows whether the working children got weekly holidays or not.

Table 6.30: Whether the Child Workers Got Weekly Holidays?

S.No.	*Whether they got weekly holidays?*	*No. of Respondents*	*Percentage*
1.	Yes	93	37.2
2.	No	157	62.8
	Total	**250**	**100**

Once again it was disheartening to note that a large number of working children 157 (62.8%) were not getting any weekly holidays. Around 93 (37.2%) child workers responded positively. These children were getting holidays once a week in the sense that the markets, viz. Lajpat Nagar, Paharganj, South Extension, etc. remained close on a particular day once a week. Hence the workers were not required on a particular day and in this way they got one day's off. In case of domestic help, they were not getting any weekly holidays, but most of them opined that once or twice a month, they got six seven hours break. During this break, they used to visit temple, friends or even went to watch movies., In case of the self employed workers, they had no holiday routine as such. But whenever they felt like, they did not go out for work. However, their only motive was to earn more and more and as such they avoided any kind of holidays. On the whole, we can say that whether it was the self-employed workers or the other workers, they rarely got any weekly holidays. However, there were some exceptions.

Cut in Wages

After getting information regarding holidays and rest intervals, we were eager to know whether there was any cut in the wages if the workers took leave. Answer to this query is given in Table 6.31.

Table 6.31: Whether there was a Cut in the Wages if the Child Worker Took Leave?

S.No.	Whether there was a cut?	No. of Respondents	Percentage
1.	Yes	148	59.2%
2.	No	102	40.8%
	Total	**250**	**100**

The table reveals that there was a cut in the wages for 148 (59.2%) children. However, 102 (40.8 %) working children opined that there was no cut in the wages if they took leave. These children were mostly those who were self employed. In the case of those children whose wages were cut, we found that they were those who were engaged in dhaba work, washermen, barber, cycle/ scooter mechanic and poorie making. In case of domestic help it was found that there was no cut in the wages if the workers took the leave for a day or two. But if they took leave for more than a week or so, there was a cut in their wages.

Overtime Work

In order to earn more money, the working children sometimes do overtime work. Keeping this fact in mind, we asked them whether they were doing overtime work. Their reply to this query is given in Table 6.32.

Table 6.32: Whether the Children do Overtime Work

S.No.	Whether they do overtime work?	No. of Respondents	Percentage
1.	Yes	176	70.4
2.	No	74	29.6
	Total	**250**	**100**

The above table reveals that 176 (70.4%) children were doing overtime work and the rest 74 (29.6%) were not doing overtime.

Those who were working overtime we further asked them whether they were paid for the overtime work. Out of the 176 workers, 112 (63.6%) replied positively and the rest 64 (36.4%) gave a negative reply. Most of them who got money for overtime work were those who were engaged in sequins work, glass beads roping, garland making, poorie making and cycle/scooter mechanic to some extent. Those engaged in sequins work and glass beads roping informed us that sometimes they receive bulk orders and have to complete the work in less time. If they complete the work within that specified time, they get extra money for that work.

Work During Festivals

Another related query which we put to them was whether they were made to work even during festivals. If yes, whether they are paid for it? The following table (6.33) presents the child workers opinion on the above query.

Table 6.33: Whether the Children are made to Work even During Festivals

S.No.	*Whether they worked during festivals?*	*No. of Respondents*	*Percentage*
1.	Yes	163	65.2
2.	No	87	34.8
	Total	**250**	**100**

From the table it becomes clear that a majority of working children 163 (65.2%) are made to work even during festivals. These workers mainly included the self employed workers, those engaged in garland making, poorie making, sequins work and domestic help. Even if they wanted to take leave during this period, they were not allowed. There were 87 (34.8%) child workers who did not work during the festivals. In this case, if there was shortage of manpower, then some of them were made to work and were even paid for it. Those who were made to work even during the festivals (163), we further asked them whether they were paid for this work. To this, 121 (74.2%) of them responded positively and 42 (25.8%) of them gave a negative reply. The domestic workers informed us that sometimes they are paid in cash and sometimes in kind i.e., clothes, shoes or something which the worker needs.

Facilities Lacking at Workplace

Our next query to them was what all facilities were lacking at their workplace. Their reply is presented in Table 6.34.

Table 6.34: Facilities Lacking at the Child Workers Workplace

S.No.	*Facilities Lacking at Workplace*	*No. of Respondents*	*Percentage*
1.	Spacious Rooms	28	1.2
2.	Proper Ventilation	82	32.8
3.	Safe Drinking Water	73	29.2
4.	Toilets	52	20.8
5.	Sunlight	15	6
	Total	**250**	**100**

The table shows that maximum number of working children 82 (32.8%), complained about proper ventilation. Most of these children were staying in jhuggies and were involved in sequins work and glass beads roping. Some of them were involved in cycle/scooter repair work and some were barbers. The barbers and the cycle/scooter mechanics had to work in such places where there was no proper ventilation. A sizeable number of working children 73 (29.2%), complained about safe drinking water. They said due to this water problem they get ill and cannot go to work. As a result, there is a cut in their wages. Another group of children 52 (20.8%), complained about the toilets. They opined that toilets were very dirty and many a times they had to use the open space. There were some other children 28 (1.2%), especially the barbers and scooter/cycle mechanic who opined that they were not having spacious rooms to work. They had to work in a very small and congested place. Still some other children 15 (6%), complained that they do not get proper sunlight.

Besides these, many children, especially those who were working in open space complained that they have to bear the heat wave in summers, rains in rainy season and cold wind in winters. The mehandi appliers sitting at Hanuman Mandir, Baba Kharag Singh Marg, especially complained about this problem. Due to this problem they can not earn much. Even the shoe-shine boys, the rag pickers working at Lajpat Nagar and South Extension complained about this problem.

Extra Benefits

Further we wanted to know from them whether they were getting any extra benefits other than salary. The following table (6.35) gives the details of the benefits the child workers were getting.

Table 6.35: Benefits which the Child Workers were Receiving other than Salary

S.No.	*Extra Benefits*	*No. of Respondents*	*Percentage*
1.	Medical Care	-	-
2.	Transport Facility	-	-
3.	Food	92	36.8
4.	House	85	34
5.	None	73	29.2
	Total	**250**	**100**

We can see from the table that 92 (36.8%) working children were getting food besides their salary. These children were mostly dhaba workers and those engaged in poorie making, domestic help and garland making. Other 85 (34%) of them were provided accommodation facility besides the salary. These workers were dhaba workers and those engaged in domestic help, poorie making, garland making and to some extent washermen and shoe keepers. There were some other children 73 (29.2%), who were not getting anything except salary. These children were rag pickers, mehandi appliers, cycle/scooter mechanic, barbers, hawkers and those engaged in sequins work and glass beads roping.

Treatment Given By Employers

Our next query to them was regarding the treatment which they were getting from their employers. The treatment which was given to them is presented in Table 6.36.

The above table reveals that the children were getting a very bad treatment from their employers. 105 (42%) children complained that their employer used to scold them for every small fault and sometimes without any reason. Some others 92 (36.8%), complained about being beaten up by their masters. Still some others 53 (21.2%), said that their was a cut in their salary if they did any mistake. So far as the self employed workers are concerned, though they were not having any master, still they were also facing similar problems. They were being beaten up and scolded by the police. Some times they even had to pay *hafta* (weekly amount) to them.

Table 6.36: Treatment Given to the Child Workers by their Employers

S.No.	*Treatment by the Employer*	*No. of Respondents*	*Percentage*
1.	Beating	92	36.8
2.	Scolding	105	42
3.	Not Giving Salary	53	21.2
4.	None	-	-
	Total	250	100

We further asked the child workers whether their employer listened to their grievances. Table 6.37 shows the employers concern towards the child workers.

Table 6.37: Grievances of the Child Workers Listened by their Employers

S.No.	*Grievances Listened*	*No. of Respondents*	*Percentage*
1.	Sometimes	120	48
2.	Always	25	10
3.	Rarely	55	22
4.	Never	50	20
	Total	250	100

From the table it becomes clear that in the case of 120 (48%) children, their employers listened to their grievances sometimes. Only 25 (10%) children said that their masters always listened to their grievances. These children were mostly those who were engaged in glass beads roping and sequins work. 5 (22%) of them opined that their grievances were heard rarely and 50 (20%) children complained that their grievances have never been heard. Whenever they have any problem, their employer says either you work with your problems or you can leave the job. Some times they do not have any alternative but to do the work. If they try to switch over to some new place, they initially get less salary and in a way they are the losers.

Satisfaction with the Job

Our next query was whether they were satisfied with their job. The following table (6.38) shows the satisfaction level of the workers.

Table 6.38: Whether the Child Workers were Satisfied with their Job?

S.No.	Whether satisfied with their job?	No. of Respondents	Percentage
1.	Yes	193	77.2
2.	No	57	22.8
	Total	250	100

The table reveals that 193 (77.2%) children were satisfied with their job whereas 57 (22.8%) were not satisfied. Those who where satisfied said that at least they are earning and helping their parents. Though sometimes they do not feel like working because of the beating/scolding by their employers. Yet they are satisfied that they are not sitting idle. Those who gave a negative reply opined that the working environment is not good and they face lots of problem while working. Hence they are not satisfied with their job.

After knowing whether they are satisfied or not, we asked them the extent of satisfaction, which is presented in Table 6.39.

Table 6.39: The Extent to which the Child Workers were Satisfied

S.No.	Satisfaction to What Extent	No. of Respondents	Percentage
1.	Very Much	36	14.4
2.	Somewhat	157	62.8
3.	Not at all	57	22.8
	Total	250	100

We can see that a majority of children 157 (62.8 %) were somewhat satisfied with their job and only 36 (14.4%) of them were very much satisfied with the job. There were 57 (22.8%) other children who were not at all satisfied with their job.

Some organised gangs use the children for pick pocketing. Accordingly, we asked them whether they were aware of them. We were surprised to note that none of the child workers (250) were aware about the pick pocketing gangs. We further asked them whether they were caught pick pocketing by the police. Once again we got a similar response. All the respondents (250) gave a negative reply. They said we were never caught by the police for pick pocketing.

Children Engaged for Immoral Traffic

Some people engage children for immoral traffic. We asked the working children whether they were aware of this. Their answer is presented in Table 6.40 given below.

Table 6.40: Awareness of the Child Workers about the Gangs which Engaged Children in Immoral Traffic

S.No.	*Children's Awareness*	*No. of Respondents*	*Percentage*
1.	Yes	73	29.2
2.	No	177	70.8
	Total	**250**	**100**

The table shows that 73 (29.2%) children were aware about the gangs which engaged children in immoral traffic. On the other hand, 177 (70.8%) of them were not aware about these kinds of gang. Those who gave a positive reply (73), we further asked them whether they have fallen in such trap. To this all of them said no. They said though we are aware about these gangs but we have not fallen in such trap.

Future Plan

Our last and final query to them was regarding their future plan as every human being has a desire for the future life. Table 6.41 shows the future plan of the child workers.

The above table reveals that majority of working children 86 (34.4%) expressed their desire to join some other work. This is a clear indication of informal sector workers as generally, people working in informal sectors do not stay in a particular job for a long time. Similarly, the working children of NCT of Delhi also want to change their job from time to time. On the other hand, 68 (27.2%) of them expressed their desire to remain in the same work as they have learnt the work and are also satisfied with it. Some of

Table 6.41: Future Plan of the Child Workers

S.No.	Future Plan	No. of Respondents	Percentage
1.	To remain in the same work	68	27.2
2.	To join some other work	86	34.4
3.	Quit the work and start studying	10	4
4.	To get technical training	56	22.4
5.	Whatever parents say	20	8
6.	Do not know	10	4
	Total	**250**	**100**

the child workers 56 (22.4%) had the desire of getting technical training so that they can earn more after this training. Some 20 (8%) children wanted that their future plan should be decided by their parents. Whereas only 10 (4%) wanted to study further and a similar percentage of them did not have any future aim.

Summing Up

After going through this empirical analysis we can say that in the NCT of Delhi, a large percentage of children start working at a very young age because of several factors like broken families, alcoholic parents, aversion towards education, a desire to supplement family income and other problems. These children are engaged in various vocations like rag picking, glass beads roping, sequins work, dhaba /road side café workers, domestic help, shoe shine boys, shoe keeping, garland making, poorie making, hawkers, washermen, barbers and cycle/scooter mechanics. Their area of operation is not confined rather spread throughout Delhi. Most of the work done by them are monotonous, repetitive and dull in nature. Their wages depend entirely on the work they do. The child is paid much less that what an adult earns for the same work. These children have no health security measures and are exposed to extreme weather conditions, traffic hazards, police beating, besides becoming victims of unhealthy habits like smoking, drinking, gutka chewing, etc. These children have very little contact with their parents as most of them were runaways and had no contact with their parents. Even those who stayed with their parents have less contact with them because the parents have no time to care for them. Those who were runaways stay either on pavements, or in the place of their work, or the railway platforms or in the shelter homes provided by the NGOs like Salam Balak Trust and Prayas. A greater percentage of these children were school drop outs and illiterates. The reason behind this is that they have aversion towards education because there is no one to guide them. Even their parents think that educating them will be of no help and as such send their children to do work. Some of the working children were getting non formal education, besides their work. Thus, if the child workers are given vocational training, they can take up skilled jobs in future and can earn more money.

7

Field Notes and Recommendations

We have already mentioned in the methodology that apart from serving the written schedule, we also followed the method of observation and maintained the field diary during the field work. During the course of field work, we observed some striking facts about the child labour. When we talked to Government officials to provide some data on child labour, their reply was that there was no data available with them because as per government records there was no child labour in Delhi. But our empirical findings suggest something different and bring out some revealing facts about the child labour.

Before conducting the survey we moved in all the four areas of Delhi i.e., North, South, West and East and tried to locate the children engaged in various informal sectors. It was our sincere endeavor to make the sample a representative one and present a realistic picture. Though we had to cross many a hurdles during the field work and intervention by the employers of the children, yet we succeeded in our mission. Sometimes it so happened that the person who had engaged the child did not allow us to talk to the child. In that case we noted the address of the boys/girls and lured them to come to some isolated place on one pretext or the other. In this way we were able to get the desired information from the children.

The child workers were divided in various categories like rag pickers, dhaba workers, cycle and scooter repairing work, garland making and poori/kachori making, shoe-shining, vending, domestic help, working as washerman, hair cutting, shoe keeping, mehandi applying, glass beads roping etc. Similarly, from all the four zones of Delhi, areas covered for the field work are as follows: New Delhi Railway Station, Lajpat Nagar, Paharganj, Yamuna Pushta, Naglamachi Pragati Maidan Jhuggi, Sarai Kale Khan,

Hanuman Mandir, Baba Kharag Singh Marg, Prachin Hanuman Mandir near Yamuna Bazar, Inter-State Bus Terminal, Mayur Vihar, South Extension and Shadi Pur Depot.

Our observation of the child workers of various categories are as follows.

Rag Pickers

For rag pickers we selected basically three areas i.e New Delhi Railway Station, Lajpat Nagar and South Extension. It was very striking that on the railway station all the rag pickers interviewed were the boys between the age group of 7-14 years whereas in Lajpat Nagar and South Extension all were the girls between the age group of 5-12. On Railway Station what we observed that the boys were waiting patiently for arrival of the trains and no sooner the train reached on the platform, they entered into different compartments and started collecting the empty plastic bottles of water, newspapers and magazines which the passengers deliberately left in the compartment. This was the routine not only for the day but night trains also. The boys were either fled from their native place of Bihar, Uttar Pradesh or Orissa or do not live with their parents in Delhi. These children may also be called parentless children inspite of the fact that their parents were alive but without caring for the child either the mother married to somebody else or the father lived with some other lady. Therefore, the railway platform was their home, their earth and everything. Some boys had their night shelter on the first floor of the GRP Police Thana, where an NGO called Salam Balak Trust runs its non-formal education system. Of late in this contact point girls have also started living. The management of the NGO appear to be good but due to the mixed nature of children staying there create some problem. It was also observed that young boys between the age group of 12-15 worked in a combined way. We also noticed that some of them fill the empty bottles of mineral water at the station itself and seal it with some very small machine and again sell it to the passengers in the name of mineral water. Though they used to earn a good income but almost 95 per cent of them are addicts. Some of them frankly admitted that they take country liquor regularly. They also admitted that in Paharganj there is a stationery shop which sells country liquor at the rate of

Rs. 20 per 'thaili' (pouch). Remaining of them were addict of gutka chewing mixed with tobacco. This habit was noticed even among the children of age group 6-12. The girls were also in habit of chewing gutka.

In rag picking the boys have contact with some adult male through whom they sell the rag and the contact man also gets commission. On the whole, inspite of good earning their physical condition was very pitiable and some had developed cough.

The girl rag pickers who were engaged in Lajpat Nagar and South Extension were basically from Tamil Nadu and Assam. They used to move in groups under the leadership of some elderly lady. They admitted that their weekly income by rag picking was somewhere near Rs. 250-Rs. 300. They support their guardians. They basically live in Sarai Kale Khan, Nizammudin and Jal Vihar area and from there, they go to Lajpat Nagar and South Extension at 8.00 a.m. that too on foot and come back to their house/jhuggi by 9.30 p.m. They assemble for their lunch in the park of the Lajpat Nagar and South Extension market at 2.00 p.m. and after taking the lunch again get busy with the routinised work. Some of them were moving with their mothers who were also engaged in rag picking work. It was noticed that some of them were in habit of gutka chewing and smoking bidi. The girls admitted that upto the age of 12 they are engaged in rag picking but after attaining the age of 13 they were engaged as domestic help in various colonies situated nearby. Sometimes they fall in trap of bad elements and get molested.

If we compare the rag pickers from boys and girls category, we find that the girls start picking rag at an early age. Secondly, the most striking thing was that the boy rag pickers had no parents and home to stay whereas 95 per cent of girls stayed with their parents. Income wise too the boys earned more in comparison to girls. But so far as saving is concerned, the girls saved more than the boys. It is because the boys have no parental control and whatever they earn, they spend it on their food, clothes, liquor, gutka and watching movies. The boys after attaining adulthood joined the coolie's rank as their profession and got married.

Cycle, Scooter, Motor Mechanic and Welding Work

A sizeable number of sample male children were engaged as cycle, scooter, motor mechanic and welding work. The areas covered during the survey include Yamuna Pushta, Sarai Kale Khan, Paharganj, Laxmi Nagar and Shadipur Depot. Actually, they are doing very hard work as their working hour was from 8.00 a.m. to 9.00 p.m. without any rest except sparing some time for lunch. Mostly they were homeless and prefer to stay in the garage or shop itself even during the night. Their appearance was very dirty and were living in a very unhygienic environment. Their income varied from Rs. 10 to Rs. 100 a day. Actually the boys who were learning the trade used to get Rs. 10 and Rs. 20 as per their quantity of work. Those who were semi-skilled they used to get Rs. 30 to Rs. 50 a day and the skilled ones got maximum Rs. 100 a day. The boys engaged in this type of work were mostly in the age group of 8-16 years. They had developed the bad habits like smoking bidi, chewing gutka and in the night taking country liquor. 50 per cent of their earning, they spend on themselves and the remaining 50 per cent, they handed over to their guardians. One very striking case of cycle/scooter repair workers we observed in Yamuna Pushta area. A boy of 12 years admitted before the research team that he gets Rs. 50 a day which comes to Rs. 1,500 per month out of which he hands over Rs. 1,000 to his parents, Rs. 200 for his personal use and remaining Rs. 300 he sends to his grandparents, who are living at his native place in Bihar. The boy appeared to be very simple and having no bad habits. His only aspiration was that after sometime if parents help him, he will start his own cycle/scooter repair shop.

Yet another eye opener case during the field visit came to our notice was that of a boy who was only 13 years. He was engaged in welding work at a very young age. He narrated the facts as to how he was forced to join this work. Actually his father was engaged in this work in the same shop in Yamuna Pushta area, but unfortunately while welding something, his entire face burned and he became blind. There was no body in the family to support. Therefore, finding no option, he stepped into the shoes of his father and started welding work to maintain the family. He further narrated that he earns that much that two square meals are provided to the family. But he has always this apprehension that like his father he may not turn blind at a very young age.

One case of beating was observed in Paharganj area, where a boy aged 8 years was working at a scooter repair shop. He had joined the trade three months back and was in the process of learning the trade. He hails from Bihar. One of his relatives had brought him to Delhi luring him to set him in a good job. Now he is learning the scooter mechanic skill. But during the course of working, on some occasion, out of ignorance, he destroys some material for which the shop keeper gives him thrashing and cuts the amount for the material destroyed from his salary. Seeing all these pathetic cases, we are surprised as to how the administration claims that there is no child labour in Delhi.

Dhaba Workers and Road Side Café

We observed that a sizeable number of children below the 14 years of age are engaged in dhabas and road side café. Ninety per cent of the dhaba workers belonged to Bihar and more than sixty per cent had fled away from their native place in search of a glamorous and happy life in Delhi. But after coming over to Delhi, either they are street children or engaged in some small work which is neither desirable nor suited to their age group. The condition of dhaba workers is more pitiable than other type of working children. They start working since 6.00 a.m. in the morning and work till mid-night and that too for Rs. 700-1,500 plus food and shelter.

If one looks at their hands and feet, tears roll in the eyes. They are inhumanly treated and often beated for breaking the crockery and not washing the cooking utensils properly. Their feet had swelled up and skin of their palms turned white. But the boys have got accustomed to such type of problems as they have not only to maintain themselves but also to support the family.

In Paharganj, opposite the New Delhi Railway Station, there are a number of dhabas in lanes and sublanes and one can easily notice three-four children working in dhaba. They hardly get half an hour rest during the afternoon for lunch and in the night, after cleaning the utensils and crockery, they retire to bed in the dhaba itself and again the same chores begin around 6.00 or 7.00 a.m. in the morning. These dhabha working children are also addicts of gutka and country liquor pouches inspite of the fact that they are very small. Here one can say that rules and laws exist only on paper and they are hardly implemented in the proper sense of the term. For example, rules clearly provide that no intoxicant can be sold to children who are below 18 years of age. But in practice even the ten years old working child goes to the stationery shop and gets illegally sold country liquor and other intoxicants. It is our presumption that under the influence of intoxicants, these boys work for such long hours and spoil their life before getting adulthood. A peculiar phenomena among these dhaba workers was noticed that they never work for more than six months or a year in one dhaba. The moment the shop keepers cut their salaries for breaking the crockerys and not cleaning the utensils properly, the boys leave the dhaba and join some other dhaba.

These children are also engaged in road side tea-stalls or in some corner of important markets. For example, we noticed two boys in the age group of 8-11 years, running a tea-stall in the courtyards of Lajpat Nagar market. Actually the capital in the tea stall was invested by someone else and the boys were asked to run the tea-stall and give 50 per cent of the daily income to the person who had provided them the tea-stall. Both of them belonged to Tamil Nadu and while making tea they smoked bidi in full public view. For entertainment they had a two-in-one music system put under the table and played music while preparing the tea. By rotation one boy will prepare the tea and the other one will supply the tea to different shops in the market from where they will get orders. This type of tea-stalls was visible on both sides of the road at certain distance in and near the market.

In Yamuna Pushta area also boys of this age group were not only running the tea-shops but also prepared 'pakoras' and other eatables. In Yamuna Pushta by and large that was the family shop where both the parents and children worked by rotation. Near Rajghat it was also observed that some very small boys were having readymade tea kettle in one hand and paper glass in other and selling the tea to the visitors coming to Rajghat. Thus, it may be concluded that the deeper one goes into the problem of child labour, the more revealing facts come to notice and therefore claiming that child labour has been abolished from NCT of Delhi is just for public consumption.

Garland and *Poorie* Making and Shoe Keepers

At both the Hanuman Mandirs i.e., one in Connaught Place and the other, Prachin Hanuman Mandir at Yamuna Bazar, number of boys were seen preparing garlands for offering, keeping shoes of the devotees and preparing *poorie/kachori*. Especially on Tuesdays and Saturdays there was big rush of devotees and they had good income, though they had to work from 4 a.m. in the morning to 1 a.m. in the next morning. These children were especially runaway children from their homes. Some of the boys engaged in garland making and poorie/kachori making admitted that they work only for two days i.e. Tuesdays and Saturdays and that too from 4 a.m. in the morning till the dead of night. In two days they earn somewhere between Rs. 250-Rs. 300, which is enough for their own maintenance. But these children may be called spoiled children as they have become addicts of ganja and charas smoking. Most of their money, is spent on ganja and charas. Some of the boys revealed the fact that from Hanuman Mandir to Bangla Sahib Gurudwara, it was a den of ganja and charas business. When asked as to who were the persons engaged in such business, their reply was the boys among themselves who got adulthood give up garland making and poorie/kachori making and engage in such business. It is all in full view of police and as reported by them, police gets 'hafta' from them. It is striking that two-three working children, during the course of interview itself, picked one cigarette from their pockets, removed the tobacco from it, mixed the ganja and again fill it very smoothly in the cigarette paper and smoke in the full view of the public. There are two contact points i.e. Prayas Bal Grih and Salam Balak Trust, run by respective two NGOs where the children stay during the night and they are being given non-formal education.

Near Prachin Hanuman Mandir, at Yamuna Bazar, the garland making boys were noticed small in numbers but shoe keepers were in large numbers. Some of them admitted that they either live in Shahdara or Yamuna Pushta with their parents and come for this work only on Tuesday and Saturday and earn between Rs. 200-Rs. 300 a day. Rest of the day, some of them either go to school, or engage in hawking work, moving from one street to another and selling something or the other. However, in this area, the number of intoxicant addict children was small.

A visible thing in regard to poverty was noticed at both the Hanuman Mandirs. We observed that on Tuesday and Saturday, many of the families alongwith their children from Laxmi Nagar and other areas come to these temples and engaged in begging both eatables and money as also taking prasad and food stuff from devotees. When asked, the ladies admitted that collection of food stuff from devotees on these two days was enough for eating for the whole week. But for that they have also to bear the pain of police 'danda'. The scene in regard to beggary on religious places forces one to believe that perhaps poverty will never disappear from India. It is really heart tearing to see small kids begging on a public place with either no clothes or torn clothes on their bodies. This is more amazing in the sense that if this is the situation of National Capital, what would be the condition in other towns and cities.

Glass Bead Roping

In Yamuna Pushta, it was a common thing to watch children roping glass beads and helping their parents. They were in age group 5 to 14 especially the girl child. When asked to their parents as to whether they have their own business, their reply was in negative. However, they themselves explained the facts to the Research Team that the contract man comes to our jhuggis with glass beads (moti) and thin wires and distributes it to those families who are interested in this work and after a week or so, he comes again to collect the prepared beads for which he pays Rs. 50 for roping 1,000 beads and Rs. 25 for 500 beads. When enquired as to how much time it takes in preparing 1,000 beads, in reply they mentioned that it depended on labour. For example, if the boys and girls work for the whole day, they can prepare 1,000 beads each. But since they were small children, they also required some time for recreation and play. Therefore, on an average they prepare, 300 to 400 beads easily. The elderly ladies of the family were also engaged in that work and they prepare 1,000 beads a day. A deeper probe as to why all of them are engaged in the job, their reply was that the earning of the male member of the family was not sufficient. Therefore, they were compelled to engage themselves in such activity.

In the Yamuna Pushta area itself particularly in Muslim populated jhuggi, fixing salma sitara on the sarees and ladies suits was very common. In this too both the small children and ladies were engaged. The procedure had been same that the contract man supply the cloth for sarees and suits, salma sitara and wire threads and also provides the design. On the basis of that design, both the children and the elderly ladies will complete the embroidery work. On an average, two girls and one lady will prepare two designer sarees or suits in a day for which they are paid Rs. 50 for each saree. Though the entire family was engaged as wage earner, yet their living condition did not reflect that they were hand to mouth because they had an electric connection in their jhuggi as also the coloured T.V. set and some other luxury goods. They frankly admitted that they were not hand to mouth, rather after spending for the whole month, they saved something also for the future. In these jhuggis there were five-six meat shops and we saw that most of the family purchased meat for cooking. When asked, they said that they prepare meat twice a week as it appeared economical in the sense that one has not to cook the pulses and the vegetables. Thus this also reflects that their condition was not so bad.

Washerman

In the Yamuna Pushta Jhuggi itself there is a dhobi ghat. Though on this dhobi ghat, majority of workers were adult, we also observed some children in age group 10-14 working as washerman. Being tempted to their work with the permission of the elderly one, we formally interviewed those children. We were surprised to note that they were not basically, the children of the washermen, rather they were the runaway children from Bihar and eastern U.P. The boys used to live somewhere in Paharganj area and early in the morning around 6.00 a.m. they reach to the Dhobi ghat with their lunch packets and start washing the clothes as the contract boys of washerman. On Ghat they used to work from 6.00 a.m. to 4.30 p.m. for which they used to get somewhere between Rs. 1,000-Rs. 1,500 per month. It was really very hard work for small children like them, but they were satisfied with the job and said that after becoming young, they will start their own washing work and employ the children like themselves. From their statement, it appeared that child labour is not going to be stopped rather it will be a perpetual phenomena.

Shoe-Shine Boys

The shoe-shine boys were interviewed at their working places i.e. New Delhi Railway Station, Lajpat Nagar, Connaught Place and

Yamuna Pushta. All the boys working as shoe-shine were in age group 10-14 years. Like rag-pickers and dhaba workers, these boys were also runaway from their native places i.e. Bihar and Eastern Uttar Pradesh. Their house, place of stay etc., was the footpath. They usually work from 9.00 a.m. to 7.30 p.m. and earned Rs. 40 to Rs. 50 a day. From that money, they saved something and kept it with some reliable elderly persons, engaged in same profession and locality. The balance money they spend on food, gutka and other intoxicants. Some of them said that they save something as said earlier and after three-four months savings, they send it to their parents in their native places. They said that they have this much of satisfaction, that they were in their own business. However, they admitted that inspite of giving 'hafta' to police, sometimes police bitterly beats them and throw away their tool kits. Whether it materializes or not but these children had a rosy dream in their mind that after getting adulthood and from money saved, they will start their own shop on 'patri' of cheap quality of sandals, chappals, shoes, etc. What was most striking that whenever they fell ill, the other shoe-shine boys, will come to their help and take care of them, till they get partially recovered. Sometimes, they get hospitalized in general wards of the hospitals for a longer duration.

Barber

In some saloons of Daryaganj, Yamuna Pushta and Paharganj, we saw some boys between the age group of 12-15 years having good height engaged as barbers. The most striking fact to be observed was that during the course of learning, they do not get any money from their master and had to depend either on begging or supported by parents living in jhuggis. After six months or so, when they become semi-skilled they are paid Rs. 15 - Rs. 20 a day varying on the skill gained during the training period. But the boys who had become fully skilled, their earning per day was somewhere between Rs. 45 to Rs. 50. But the common striking thing among all the working children was that they had become addict of something or the other and are spoiling their childhood. Sometimes by sitting in saloons itself, they worked like contact boys for supply of 'ganja' and 'charas' to the persons living in that surrounding. In comparison to other children, they were wearing comparatively better clothes and appeared to be tidy. However, health wise they were almost similar to other working boys.

Mehandi (Henna) Appliers

At the Connaught place Hanuman Mandir and Lajpat Nagar Market, we saw some small girls sitting with their mothers and applying henna on the palms of desirous women who come to the 'mandir' or market. At Hanuman mandir they admitted that for food, they had not to bother because the devotees distribute so much food stuff that it was enough for both day and night. They were mostly from Rajasthan and pursuing it as a family traditional means of livelihood. At Hanuman Mandir they used to sit from 8.00 a.m. till midnight whereas in Lajpat Nagar Market they used to sit from 11.00 a.m. to 8.00 p.m. Income wise the children engaged in henna applying used to earn much in comparison to those of Hanuman Mandir. But the children working at Hanuman Mandir got food free of cost. Corruption is so rampant in every walk of life that the children who are working for their two square meals and to support the family have to give hafta to the employees of New Delhi Municipal Corporation as also to police personnel. They have to spend on these 'haftas' to two categories of people i.e., NDMC employees and police, around Rs. 400 per month and they are able to earn around Rs. 3,000 per month. However, they gladly admitted that during marriage season and festive occasions like Diwali, Karva Chauth, Teej, Raksha Bandhan, Bhaiya Dooj, etc., their income goes up to Rs. 5,000-Rs. 5,500 a month. Here as a social science student our concern is not the earning but at highlighting the state of affairs existing in our society. The children at this very age are supposed to spend their time reading, writing and playing but are forcefully driven into these professions to supplement the family income and become the bread earner for the family.

At Hanuman Mandir two girls admitted that they were forced into this profession due to the family condition. Their father was a drunkard and whole day and night he was staying in the house drinking country liquor, beating their mother, brothers and sisters, demanding food etc. In such a situation, they had no other alternative but to engage themselves in this traditional work.

Having full of tears in their eyes, they felt satisfied that at least by entering into the trade, at such a young age, they are able not only to maintain the family but also sending their younger brothers and sisters to school so that they may not lead the life which these two sisters were leading.

To put salt to injury they further admitted that by sitting there, they had to face so many problems, for example, some male come upto them with bad intentions and often use abusive language. The police also do excess with them. But all that they had to tolerate because they had no other means of livelihood and maintain a big family.

Hawkers

Hawking is another good source of income for the working children. But most hazardous so far their health is concerned. During the course of field work, we saw a number of small children at New Delhi Railway Station, Paharganj, selling lock, key and chains which is generally purchased by the railway passengers. In this hawking work, we observed two types of boys and girls i.e. one who had invested his/her own capital and another who were engaged on contract basis by others. As regards earnings, the hawkers who had invested their own money in the articles to be sold, had comparatively better income in comparison to the contract hawkers. The independent hawkers used to get Rs. 100 — Rs. 150 per day whereas the contract workers earned Rs. 35 - Rs. 50 a day depending upon the nature of the contract. The hawkers no doubt earned, but the strain they take during the summer sun, winter cold waves and rains in rainy season is very amazing. Whole day they move from one place to another and they spend their nights in night shelter located in Basant Lane near New Delhi Railway Station. Some of them had got habituated to sleep on the 'patri' itself. All of them were the addicts of tobacco chewing mixed gutka. Most of them had runaway from their homes in West Bengal, Uttar Pradesh and Bihar.

In Chandni Chowk and Lajpat Nagar, the hawkers used to sell handkerchief, plastic made table cloths, toys, album, etc. They are always on move and sometimes persuade the passerby to purchase their goods. Their demand originally is very high but as passerby moves forward, they follow them and start reducing the price and ultimately force the purchaser to buy it on a reasonable price. This way they earn somewhere between Rs. 100-Rs. 200 per day and after reducing the cost of the material, they save somewhere between Rs. 50 — Rs. 60 per day. They spend their nights on the lanes and sub-lanes of the areas in which they operate.

Near ITO red light such child workers may be noticed selling newspapers, soft dusters for cleaning the vehicles, coconut pieces, lemon etc. As soon as the red light stops the vehicle, they rush to the vehicle and persuade the people to buy their articles. Some of them beg also. However, they do all these things at a very great risk of their lives and all of a sudden, the red light goes and vehicles start moving. They earn somewhere between Rs. 30 — Rs. 50 per day. They start at 8.00 a.m. in the morning and stay there till 9.30 p.m. They mostly belong to the jhuggies of Yamuna Pushta and the Pragati Maidan jhuggi. They live with their parents and whatever they earn, they preserve something for their expenditure on gutka and other things and the remaining they give to their parents.

Yet another category of child hawker can be seen near India Gate during 5.00 p.m. to 12.00 p.m. They generally sell toys, balloons, balls, 'bhel-puri' and some of them ice-creams and cold drinks. Here, by selling items, they earn double in the sense that the affluent families carry their children to India Gate for pleasure sake which has advantage of children's park and whatever price they demand, the parents give to honour the wishes of the children. Thus, these hawkers during seven hours i.e. 5.00 p.m. to 12.00 p.m. earn Rs. 100 — Rs. 150 a day but of course they have to bear the pain of police 'danda' and sometimes police men also extract money.

The last category of child hawkers are those who sell the goods like pen, purse, chain, magazines, etc. from bus to bus and they are always on the move. They do not have to spend their own capital but they do it for the contractor for which they get 30 per cent of the income as labour cost. These hawkers go from one bus to another in connivance with the police for which they have to give 'hafta' to the policemen. Thus, they are able to earn somewhere between Rs. 25 — Rs 40 per day. These boys are mostly from the jhuggies of the area in which they operate.

Domestic Help

If one surveys various affluent colonies of Delhi, we will see a child working as domestic help in most of the houses. They are mostly from the jhuggies and belong to tribal areas of Bihar, Orissa, Madhya Pradesh and in certain cases from Rajasthan. There are certain agencies who run domestic help placement. The children were brought to city under the pretext that they will find lucrative job and even would be able to send some money to their family. Young children of 9 years were brought from poor families of Jharkhand and Chattisgarh and later forced to work as domestic servants many under inhuman conditions. Such type of placement services can be noticed in Lajpat Nagar, South Extension, Paschim Vihar, Model Town, Janakpuri, Pitampura and Shakarpur. The agencies are owned by the tribals or non-tribal persons coming from these areas and before handing over the child to the needy family, they take commission somewhere between Rs. 400-Rs. 2,500 depending upon the locality. They employ the children for Rs. 800-Rs. 1,200 a month excluding the food and clothes and collect the money from the family itself, out of which they take 50 per cent and the remaining money they send to the parents of the children. This racket of child workers is mushrooming in Delhi. Recently, the police rescued 15 children including 12 girls from these agencies.

The working condition of these domestic help is really pitiable. They have to work from 5.00 in the morning till 11.30 in the night. They have to clean the utensils, sweep and mop the floor, wash the clothes, bringing milk and after getting some experience from the employers, they even have to take care of kitchen work. For minor mistakes they are beaten and not provided food for the whole day.

Thus, our field observation reveals that the number of working children is increasing day by day. Of course, some voluntary organizations like Salam Balak Trust, Butterflies, Don Bosco, Prayas and others are engaged in the welfare of such working children. But their help is not enough to totally remove the child labour from the NCT of Delhi. The more the politicians and activists talk about removing the child labour, the more the number of child workers is increasing. Inspite of legislation and other things in favour of children, they have become ineffective and child labour is growing day by day in Delhi.

Recommendations

As stated, the problem of child labour is growing day by day. For its elimination we need some answer to suggest. Myron Weiner has pointed out:

In India no major groups within or outside the Government are concerned with enforcing labour laws for making education compulsory, for no particular group is moved by theological, ideological, moral or even self-interest consideration. The result is that official should prepare central and state budgets merely make incremental changes in yearly educational budgets, officials in a state education and labour ministries show no interest in tightening legislation, administrators are not inclined to enforce existing laws, state and local governments, pay little attention to elementary education and teachers sit by ideally as children drop out of their classes.

Government officials are fully aware of the international embarrassment that comes with having the world's largest population of child labourers and adult illiterate, but they ascribe the failure to achieve universal education as a result of the country's poverty rather than the government's failure.

He has emphasized the urgent need to make primary education compulsory, outlining how this has been achieved in various countries of Europe as well as in the United States of America, Japan, South Korea and Taiwan. Social Anthropologist and United Nations Volunteer, Neera Burra, in her book 'Born to Work' has stated: "If there is at all blue print for tackling the problem of child labour, it is education". We are in complete agreement with this most valid and practical suggestion because in the long run, literacy is the only solution to the problem of child labour. However, the opportunity that we had while working in the field and our close interaction with child labourers, NGOs and some of the parents living in jhuggies and the general public, made us ponder on rehabilitation strategy. Therefore, while it is unquestionable that the best way to prevent the evil of child labour from spreading its tentacles any further, is by insisting on primary education and strict family norms, we can, in practical terms, deal with the problem of child labour in three significant ways. These solutions are purely indigenous and as such perfectly suited to the conditions prevailing in our country. They are the setting up of residential camps, bridge course centres and anganwadi cum creche facilities.

We have already emphasised that child labour cannot be approached as an isolated problem. It is a complex socio-economic and demographic phenomenon which can be reduced and eradicated by multiplicity of actions, both by government and public, at social as well as individual levels. Child labour is not much meaningful where it is imparted by parents as a skill to their children in the form of socialization of new generation. But the highest concern lies where the process takes place through exploitative mechanism which consumes more energy than the child possesses and the work is done under great physical and mental strain. Unless child labour is eliminated completely, there is a need to take progressive measures aiming at regulating and humanizing child work so that the young earners could be provided with some protection against conditions that hamper their physical and mental development and deny them educational and better job opportunities. Such measures include the adoption and enforcement of protective labour laws and improvement in working conditions under better welfare facilities.

The basic reason for the child labour is poverty and therefore it must be viewed with patience and understanding. The progressive elimination of child labour is possible through improvement in the income distribution and social awakening which could be addressed to the society as a whole and not particularly to the children. The income disparity can be removed by providing better employment opportunities to the lower stratum of society through creation of more jobs, agrarian reforms, enforcement of minimum wages law, social security, pension to agricultural workers, etc. These measures make it less necessary for low income groups to rely on children for meeting subsistence requirements or for providing security for the future.

Apart from that, enforcement of universal compulsory education and the provision of training and apprenticeship schemes can play a significant role in reduction and ultimately eradication of child labour. This would not only reduce illiteracy but would also provide opportunity for skill acquisition and better employment in adulthood.

The policies in regard to child labour can be addressed at two levels viz. long term and short term. The long term strategies and policies should be aimed at improving the conditions of the society as a whole to such an extent that ultimately child labour is completely eliminated. Whereas, the short term policies and plan should be aimed at improving the working and living conditions of children so long as child labour prevails. In regard to such policies various recommendations have been made by various committees and different authors.

Child labourers are increasing in number day by day inspite of various strategies evolved and implemented in India. Child labour weakens the human resource of the country and creates for future a mass of people who are not even sufficiently productive as to earn enough to keep themselves out of poverty. The hard fact is that the poverty stricken families encourage their children to work, in order to supplement their family income. Lack of parental control and ill treatment by step parents plucks the normal growth of the children and force them to run away from home. As mentioned earlier, in field observation, the metropolis of Delhi witnesses these runaway who eventually form the child work force.

The child workers who make up the largest segments of child population and their hard labour significantly contributes to the national income of the country. But the irony is that they are denied of the basic rights to health care protection, shelter, nutrition, etc.

A close look at the issue of child labour prove that child labour is a social crime and many social factors significantly contribute to child labour. Our field observation also suggest that the parents of working children are more interested in sending their wards to work rather than school. Therefore, it is suggested that compulsory education for children should be forcefully implemented.

Housing is an important welfare measure necessary for improvement of health and efficiency of child workers. It is important because they should be properly housed to grow up as healthy citizens and contribute to the economic prosperity of the country. Lack of proper housing facilities lead to the impairment of healthy growth of the children and drag them to join the group of undesirable elements which lead to anti social and delinquent behaviour. As our study suggest most of the working children in metropolis of Delhi, either stay with their parents in one room jhuggies or on footpaths and are devoid of basic facilities like sanitation, water, electricity, etc. which results into their unhealthy development.

The NGOs can play a crucial role in creating awareness about the importance of proper housing. Efforts should also be made to provide housing facilities with necessary basic amenities for working children. During the course of our survey, it was found that two NGOs i.e., Salam Balak Trust and Prayas were doing significant work in this direction.

A multiple policy approach is necessary in dealing with the problem of working children. They have to be seen distinctly in the categories of wage earning employment, as paid family worker, as apprentices in traditional crafts and as working by school going children. Each specific category has its own peculiar problems which need to be attended comprehensively and separately.

Legal sanctions are also not stringent enough to act as a deterrent as the action against employers for employing such children. Law alone cannot solve the problem of child workers in the informal sector but there should be organizations and associations to highlight the problems and chalk out the strategy to solve them. Again a single individual or a group or one agency alone cannot solve the problem of child labour. It requires pronged approach and until and unless convergence with various departments and ministries is brought about, the eradication of this social evil will indeed remain a distant dream.

Dr. Lakshmidhar Mishra, Ex-Secretary, Ministry of Labour, Government of India, has also strongly advocated the convergence of various government departments in eradicating the problem of child labour. (See the table below)

Suggestions for Elimination of Child Labour given by Dr. Lakshmidhar Mishra

1.	Department of Education	Concerned with UEE, UPE, Operation Blackboard, NFE, DPEP, NLM/TLC
2.	Department of Women and Child Development	Concerned with implementation of ICDS
3.	Ministry of Rural Development	Concerned with a number of poverty eradication and rural employment promotion programmes such as IRDP, DWCRA, TRYSEM, DPAP, DDP, JRY, EAS, PMRY.

4.	Department of Rural Development	Concerned with rural drinking water, rural sanitation, land reforms, CAPART
5.	Ministry of Health and Family Welfare	Concerned with the management of Primary Health Centres
6.	Ministry of Labour	Concerned with formulation of Labour policy and coordination with state governments for stringent and deterrent enforcement of laws concerning the elimination of child labour.

Source: Mishra, Lakshmidhar, Child Labour in India, Oxford University Press, New Delhi, 2000, p. 7.

As regards the question of responsibility for the eradication of child labour both the government at the national and state level should have to shoulder this responsibility. The state has to take more responsibility in welfare activities. Over the years, the government has gradually shifted the responsibility onto the NGO's and private social organizations. A social problem of this magnitude needs immense supervision, wider authority and sufficient funds. The government has the necessary infrastructure, enormous manpower and substantial financial resources. The state governments should not depend entirely on central government schemes. The state governments can set up a separate department and pool resources from various sources like UNICEF, World Bank, ILO, private organizations, etc. Any action plan framed for the welfare of the children by the concerned authorities should consider the facts as to what is the average expectation of a poor Indian family from a child; socio-economic structure of the area where from the child hails; the present employment and self-employment opportunities available in urban areas; the present system of elementary and secondary education and facilities for vocational guidance or orientation and training and the plan period programmes for such activities. When it comes to implementing these vocational training for skill development and skill upgradation, it is necessary to know how much the NGOs could contribute inspite of the haphazard infrastructure and limited resources at their command. One should not ignore their role simply because they might not represent any formal governmental structure in the country.

The overall programme, of rehabilitation of child labour needs people's participation and cooperation from all sectors i.e., from their families to the societies working for them. Realization of people is very much essential by which they can think for these children exploited at different work spots. Their overall support would be helpful in achieving the objectives of rehabilitation of child labour.

However, the coordinated efforts of government and NGOs, employers and social workers through active public support can definitely help in ameliorating or controlling the problem from the state as well as from the country.

The community should be actively involved in a major way. This is absolutely necessary as they should be ready to take over and monitor the provided facilities when the original group that establishes it withdraws. Women from self help groups, members of the ward education committee and youth groups prove effective in this area of community participation. In this context the efforts made by Akansha, a Community Scheme of Salam Balak NGO, is doing a commendable job in Delhi.

Similarly, several women welfare organizations, like the army and railway officers wives are involved in welfare activities. Groups can work together but unlike convergence of government department, here the stress can be on the convergence of non-formal groups.

One of the root causes underlying many of the problems that India as a country faces is over population. Resources and infrastructure remain fixed but the number assessing it grows continuously. This creates numerous problems, be it in the area of basic necessities or better amenities. Thus, relentless growth has to be controlled by means of strict regulations and prohibitions, through family planning measures. Men especially have to be mobilized.

The aim of social policies should be to reduce the intensity of child labour and improve the quality of working condition for children in short term and finally, eradicate the child labour in long term planning.

The Supreme Court, in December 1996, while disposing of a public interest litigation, directed setting up of a Child Labour Rehabilitation Worker Fund in which employers of child worker were asked to pay a compensation of Rs. 20,000/- per child worker and suggested a number of measures to rehabilitate working children in a phased manner. The High Court said, "in the context of India, the problem persists here is really not dearth of resources but lack of real zeal. Let this not continue. Let us all put our head and efforts together and assist the child for its good and greater good of the country". The Judges hoped in the concluding parts of the judgement that the closing years of the 20th century would see that the promises made to our children by our Constitution about a half-century ago are accomplished.

The following measures may also be suggested to improve the work and living conditions to minimize the negative effects of early employment.

The protective laws on the age at employment, minimum wages, working hours, rest interval, weekly holidays, need to be enforced more vigorously. There should be a complete ban on child labour in hazardous industries.

Nutritional food and protective clothes should be provided to the working children at subsidized rates at the places of work.

The working children should have access to periodic health and medical check up and treatment through their employers.

The places of work and residence should be provided with adequate infrastructure like safe drinking water and proper sanitation facilities.

Besides, provision of gloves and other protective items to children working in the industrial units; protection of self employed children against the occupational competition with the adults, moral education and protection against mis-guidance by anti social elements; controlling the drug addiction; etc. and occupational guidance, education and recreational facilities for the working children should be taken care of.

The beggary should be totally prohibited and the children involved in beggary should be organized in such a way that apart from getting informal education, they should earn something by getting them involved in some light work and for limited hours.

The long term policies should be oriented to the eradication of poverty through employment generating policies and maintenance allowance to the needy families; the spread of school education with provision of vocational training; creating public awareness to the consequences of early employment and towards the existing laws concerning child labour; effective role of trade unions in implementing the existing laws on minimum age for entry in the labour force, minimum wages, working hours, rest interval, creating public opinion about improving the quality of environment at work and a balanced regional development on socio-economic fronts.

Bibliography

Government Documents/Reports

Annual Report of Asha Nivas Social Service Centre, Chennai, 1996-97.

Bequele, A. and Myers, W.E., First things first in Child Labour: Eliminating Work Detrimental to Children, UNICEF/ILO, Geneva, 1995.

Brochure of Arunodhaya Social Service Centre, Chennai.

Census of India, Provisional Population Total Workers and Non Workers, Paper 3 Series, India, 1981.

Child and Work, An ILO Policy Framework for the International year of Children, ILO, Geneva, February, 1978.

Child Labour, A Briefing Manual, International Labour Office, Geneva, 1986.

Gangrade, K.D., Children at Work, ILO, Geneva, 1979.

George, K.N., "Child Labour in the City of Madras," Paper presented at a National Seminar on Employment of Children in India, organized by National Institute of Public Cooperation and Child Development, New Delhi, August, 1977.

Government of India, Child in India — A statistical profile, Ministry of Welfare, New Delhi, 1985.

Government of India, Ministry of Labour, Annual Report, 1983-84, New Delhi, 1985.

Government of India, Report of the Committee on Child Labour, Ministry of Labour, New Delhi, 1979.

ILO, Child Labour: Extract from the Report of the Director—General to the International Labour Conference, 69th Session, Geneva, 1986.

ILO-IIPA Action Programme No. 090.92.325.254 on Elimination of Child Labour, Indian Institute of Public Administration, New Delhi.

ILO, IPEC Programme Document, Geneva, 1992-93.

ILO, Towards the Abolition of Child Labour: ILO Policy and its

Implications for ILO technical — cooperation activities, ILO Publication, 1993.

ILO, World Labour Report, ILO, Geneva, 1992.

IPEC Filer, International Labour Office, Geneva.

IPEC, Reflection on the Past, Pointers to the Future, ILO Office, Geneva, 1994.

Mazumdar, Dipak, The Urban Informal Sector, World Bank Staff Working Paper, No. 211, Washington, 1975.

National Institute of Human Resource Development, Labour Welfare — A tool for Industrial Peace and Productivity, Monograph, Chennai, 1990.

Report of the Director General of the International Labour Organisation, 1983.

Report of the 57th Session of the International Labour Conference, Geneva, 1972.

Shukla, B.N. and Shukla, Bimla, "Child Labour in the Informal Sector", Paper Presented at Annual Conference of the Indian Society of Labour Economics (ISLE), Bhubaneswar, 1990.

Speech of Shri G. Venkat Swamy, Former Union Minister of Textiles, Delivered at the Workshop of District Collectors/ District Heads on "Towards Eliminating Child Labour", held at Vigyan Bhawan, September 13-14, 1995.

Sukumar, David, Interpretations on Combating Child Labour, IRDS - ILO-IPEC Programme Against Child Labour, India, 1996.

The Right to be a Child, UNICEF House, New Delhi, 1994.

UNICEF, Children in Especially Difficult Circumstances, Unpublished paper for the Executive Board 1986 Session, New York, 1986.

UNICEF India, Annex to the Annual Report on Goals and Indicators, New Delhi, 1993.

UNICEF India, Background Paper, The Right to be a Child, March, 1994.

UNICEF India, Policy on Child Labour, New Delhi, 1993.

UNICEF, Informal Paper by Chairman of the Executive Board, New York, 1986.

UNICEF, The Continuing Revolution for Children, UNICEF House, New Delhi, 1995.

UNICEF, The State of the World's Children, United Nations Children's Fund, 1995.

UNICEF, The State of the World's Children — Focus on Child Labour, United Nations Children's Fund, 1997.

UNICEF, The progress of Indian States, United Nations Children's Fund, New Delhi, 1995 and 1996.

World of Work, The Magazine of ILO, No. 4, Bureau of Public Information of the ILO, Geneva, 1993.

Books

Anker, Richard, Barge, Sandhya, Rajagopal, S. and Joseph, M.P. (eds.), Economics of Child Labour in Hazardous Industries of India, Centre for Operations Research and Training, Baroda, 1998.

Arimpoor, Joe, Street Children of Madras: A Situational Analysis, National Labour Institute, Child Labour Cell, Noida, 1992.

Aziz, Abdul, Urban Poor and Urban Informal Sector, Ashish Publishing House, New Delhi, 1984.

Background Document of the UN System in India: Position Paper on Child Labour, International Labour Organisation, New Delhi, 1998.

Bhagwan, P.D. Singh and Shukla, Mahanty, Children at Work, Problems and Policy Options, B.R. Publishing Corporation, Delhi, 1993.

Bhal, Harsh, Evolving media strategy for elimination of child labour in Brassware industry of Moradabad District, APPPA Dissertation, Indian Institute of Public Administration, New Delhi, 2002 (unpublished).

Bhargava, Pramila H., The Elimination of Child Labour Whose Responsibility?, Sage Publications, New Delhi, 2003.

Bhattacharya, Sheba, Child Labour and Education, Case Study in Delhi, APPPA Dissertation, Indian Institute of Public Administration, New Delhi, 2002-03 (Unpublished).

Bjorkman, James Warner, The Changing Division of Labour in South Asia, Manohar Publications, New Delhi, 1987.

Burra, Neera, Born to work: Child Labour in India, Oxford University Press, Delhi, 1995.

Chakravarty, B., Education and Child Labour, Chugh, Allahabad, 1989.

Chandra Mowli, V., Jogin — Girl Child Labour Studies, Sterling Publishers, New Delhi, 1992.

Child Labour: Challenge and Response: A Status Report on Indian Initiatives Towards the Elimination of Child Labour, V.V. Giri National Labour Institute, Noida, 1996.

Child Labour Law — An Overview, Child Labour Legal Studies Cell, V.V. Giri National Labour Institute, Noida, 1998.

Child Labour Series, Working Children in India, Child Labour Cell, Noida, December, 1993.

Dandekar, K., Child Labour — Do Parents Count It As An Economic Aspect of the Child in India, Himalaya Publishing House, Bombay, 1979.

D'Lima, Hazel and Gosalia, Rima, Street Children of Bombay: A Situational Analysis, National Labour Institute, Child Labour Cell, Noida, 1992.

Desai, A.R. and Devadas Pillai, S., Slums and Urbanisation, Popular Prakashan, Bombay, 1970.

Devi, Laxmi, Encyclopaedia of Child and Family Welfare, Vol. 4, Institute for Sustainable Development, Lucknow and Anmol Publications, New Delhi, 1998.

Fernandes, Walter and Thukral, Enakshi Ganguly, Development Displacement and Rehabilitation, Indian Social Institute, New Delhi, 1989.

Fyfe, Alec, Child Labour: A Guide to Project Design, International Labour Office, Geneva, 1993.

Fyfe, Alec, Child Labour, Polity Press, Cambridge, 1989.

Gangrade, K.D., Child Labour in India, Department of Social Work, University of Delhi, Delhi, 1978-79 (Unpublished).

Gangrade, K.D. and Gandhi, J.A., Women and Child Workers in Unorganised Sector, Concept Publishing Company, Delhi, 1983.

George, Ivy, Child Labour and Child Work, Ashish Publishing House, New Delhi, 1990.

Ghosh, A., Street Children of Calcutta: A Situational Analysis, National Labour Institute, Child Labour Cell, Noida, 1992.

Ghosh, Ashish and Sekar, Helen R., Child Labour in Moradabad home based industries in the wake of legislation, National Labour Institute, Noida, 2000.

Jain, Mahaveer, Child Labour in India — A Select Bibliography, National Labour Institute, Noida, 1994.

Joseph, M.P., IPEC in India 1992-95, Looking Back, ILO, New Delhi, 1996.

Joshi, Preeta, International Labour Organisation and its Impact on India, B.R. Publishing Corporation, New Delhi, 1985.

Jyothi, P.T., Lost Childhood, Don Bosco Anbu Illam, Chennai, 1995.

Kalpagam, U., Labour and Gender — Survival in Urban India, Sage, New Delhi, 1994.

Kanbargi, Ramesh (ed.), Child Labour in the Indian Subcontinent: Dimensions and Implications, Sage, New Delhi, 1991.

Khan, M.A., Sociological Aspects of Child Development, Concept Publishing Company, New Delhi, 1979.

Kudamala, Sreeramamurty, Urban Labour in Informal Sector, B.R. Publishing Corporation, Delhi, 1986.

Kulshreshtha, Jinesh Chandra, Child Labour in India, Ashish, New Delhi, 1978.

Kulshreshtha, Jinesh Chandra, Indian Child Labour, Uppal, New Delhi, 1994.

Kumar, Bimal, Structural Basis of Child Labour, Concept Publishing, New Delhi, 1994.

Mangold, G.B., Problems of Child Labour, Macmillan Company, New York, 1970.

Mathew, P.M., Informal Sector in India:Critical Perspectives, Khama Publishers, New Delhi, 1995.

Mishra, Lakshmidhar, Child Labour in India, Oxford University Press, New Delhi, 2000.

Mishra, Lakshmidhar, Jain, Mahaveer and Mohsin, Nadeem, Report on National Seminar on Implementation of Child Labour Projects, Published by National Resource Centre on Child Labour, V. V. Giri National Labour Institute, Noida, 1997.

Moddie, A.D., The Concept of Work in Indian Society, Indian Institute of Advanced Study and Manohar Publications, New Delhi, 1990.

Mustafa, Mohd. and Sharma, Onkar, Child Labour in India: A Bitter Truth, Deep and Deep, New Delhi, 1996.

Naidu, Usha S. and Kapadia, Kamini R., Child Labour and Health Problems and Prospects, S. Krishnamoorthy for Tata Institute of Social Sciences, Bombay, 1985.

Pachal, Tapan Kumar, Child Labour in Bulandshahar District of Uttar Pradesh, National Labour Institute, Noida, 2000.

Pandhe, M.K., Child Labour in India, India Book Exchange, Calcutta, 1979.

Panicker, Rita and Nangia, Praveen, Working and Street Children of Delhi, National Labour Institute, Child Labour Cell, Noida, 1992.

Pati, R.N., Rehabilitation of Child Labourers in India, Ashish Publishing House, New Delhi, 1990.

Patil, B.R., Working Children in Urban India, D.B. Publishers, Bangalore, 1988.

Ramanujam, M.S., et.al., Employment in the Informal Sector (A Study of Selected Towns), Agricole Publishing Academy for Institute of Applied Manpower Research, New Delhi, 1994.

Rao, B.V., Socio-economic Change in Belgaum District (A Historical Probing), Himalaya Publishing House, Bombay, 1989.

Rao, B.V.R and Mallik, B., Street Children of Hyderabad: A Situational Analysis, National Labour Institute, Child Labour Cell, Noida, 1992.

Rawat, B.D., India in ILO, RBSA Publishers, Jaipur, 1990.

Reddy, N., Street Children of Bangalore: A Situational Analysis, National Labour Institute, Child Labour Cell, 1992.

Rodgers, Garry and Standing, Guy (eds), Child Work, Poverty and Under-development, ILO, Geneva, 1981.

Satya Raju, R., Urban Unorganised Sector in India, Mittal Publications, Delhi, 1989.

Saxena, R.C., Labour Problems and Social Welfare, Jai Prakash Nath and Co. Publishers, Meerut, 1952.

Shah, Nazir Ahmed, Child Labour in India, Anmol Publications, New Delhi, 1992.

Sharma, B.K. and Mittar, Vishwa, Child Labour and Urban Informal Sector, Deep and Deep, New Delhi, 1990.

Singh, A.N., Child Labour in India, Socio-Economic Perspectives, Shipra Publications, Delhi, 1990.

Singh, A.N. The Child Rag-pickers Socio-Economic Perspectives and Intervention Strategies, Shipra Publications, Delhi, 1996.

Singh, I.S., Child Labour, Oxford and IBH, New Delhi, 1992.

Singh, Manjit, Labour Process in the Unorganised Industry, Indian Institute of Advanced Study, Shimla, Manohar Publications, New Delhi, 1991.

Singh, S.D. and Pothen, K.P., Slum Children of India, Deep and Deep Publications, New Delhi, 1982.

Sinha, Swapan Kumar, Child Labour in Calcutta: A Sociological Study, P.S. Basu Naya Prakash, Calcutta, 1991.

Sreenivasan, M.A., Labour in India, Vikas Publishing House, Delhi, 1980.

Study of Child Labour in Bombay, National Institute of Public Cooperation and Child Development, New Delhi, 1978, (Unpublished).

Sumangala, M. and Nagarajan, B.S., Economics of Child Labour and Fertility, B.R. Publishing Corporation, Delhi, 1993.

Summary of UNICEF's the State of the World's Children, Oxford University Press, 1996.

Thakur, R.N., Chaubey, P.K. and Narain, M.K., ILO — IIPA Training Workshop for NCLP Project Directors on Elimination of Child Labour, April 12-23, 1999, Indian Institute of Public Administration, New Delhi, 1999.

The State of the World's Children, Published for UNICEF by Oxford University Press, 1997.

Towards Eliminating Child Labour: A Report of the Workshop of District Collectors/District Heads, V.V. Giri National Labour Institute, National Resource Centre on Child Labour, Noida, 1996.

Tripathy, S.K., Child Labour in India, Discovery Publishing House, New Delhi, 1989.

Tripathy, S.N., Child Labour in India — Issues and Policy Options, Discovery Publishing House, New Delhi, 1996.

Varandani, Gursharan, Child Labour and Women Workers, Ashish Publishing House, New Delhi, 1994.

Vidyasagar, R., Chandra, K. Suman and Reddy, Y. Gangi, Child Labour in State industry of Markapur in the wake of Legislation, National Labour Institute, Noida, 2000.

Visaria, Pravin and Jacob, Paul, Child Labour in India — Results of a Methodological Survey in Surrendranagar and Surat Districts of Gujarat State, Gujarat Institute of Development Research, Ahmedabad, 1995.

Visaria, Pravin and Unni, Jeemol, Self-employed Women Population and Human Resource Development, Gujarat Institute of Development Research, Ahmedabad, 1995.

Weiner, Myron, The Child and State in India: Child Labour and Education Policy in Comparative Perspective, Oxford University Press, Delhi, 1991.

Articles in Journals/Magazines/Newspapers

"A future without Child Labour", Indian Journal of Labour Economics, Vol. 45, No. 3, July-September, 2002

"A Gesture to Children Working in Metal Factories", The Hindu, 24 November, 1994.

Agarwal, Abha, "Child Labour in Glass Industry", Yojana, Vol. 42, No. 12, December, 1998.

Ahmed, Iftikhar, "Getting Rid of Child Labour", Economic and Political Weekly, Vol. 34, No. 27, 3 July, 1999.

Ahuja, Daman, "Politics of Child Labour', Social Welfare, Vol. 48, No. 8, November, 2001.

Alam, Jayanti, "Child Labour: Need to Change the Adult Mindset", Social Change, Vol. 27, Nos. 3-4, September-December, 1997.

Anandharaja Kumar, P., "Child Labour in India: Causes and Consequences", Third Concept, Vol. 11, Nos. 122-23, April-May, 1997.

Anandharaja Kumar, P., "Child Labour: Issues and Solution", Kurukshetra, Vol. 47, No. 10, July, 1999.

Anandharaja Kumar, P., "Working on the Street: Bitter Present, Bleak Future", Social Welfare, Vol. 46, No. 8, November, 1999.

"Autonomous Agency Proposed for Child Labour Eradication," The Hindu, 25 August, 1996.

Awards Digest, Journal of Labour Legislation, Vol. XX, No. 7-12, July-December, 1994.

"Awareness Campaign Against Child Labour", The Hindu, 31 May, 1995.

Babu, K.S., "Working Children in Jaipur's Gem Industry", Social Welfare, Vol. 46, No. 8, November, 1999.

Bajpai, Asha, "Child Labour: 'Fond Hopes' for the Future", Indian Journal of Social Work, Vol. 58, No. 4, October, 1997.

Balasubramanian, N.S., "Urban Employment in Unorganised Sector," Yojana, June, 1984.

Basu, Dipak, "Lost Childhood", Statesman, 4-5 February, 2002.

Basu, Kaushik, "Child Labour: Cause, Consequence, and Cure, with Remarks On International Labour Standards", Journal of Economic Literature, Vol. 37, No. 3, September, 1999.

Basu, Kaushik and Van, Phan Hoang, "The Economics of Child Labour", American Economic Review, Vol. 88, No. 3, June, 1998.

Bequele, Assefa and Boyden, Jo, "Combating Child Labour", Condition of Work Digest, Vol. 10, No. 1, 1991, Part II, Annex 3, ILO, Geneva, 1995.

"Better deal sought for Working Children", The Hindu, I May, 1996.

Bhargava, Pramila H., "Practical Solution to the Child Labour Problem," Kurukshetra, Vol. 49, No. 4, January, 2001.

Bhaskar, Mini, "Child Labour: How the Law has Evolved?", Social Change, Vol. 27, Nos. 3-4, September-December, 1997.

Bhatty, Kiran, "Child Labour: Breaking the Vicious Cycle," Economic and Political Weekly, Vol. 31, No. 7, 17 February, 1996.

Buddhapriya, Sanghamitra, "Child Labour: The Victim of Exploitation", Yojana, Vol. 39, No. 8, June, 1995.

Buddhapriya, Sanghamitra, "Role of Primary Education in Tackling the Problem of Child Labour", Kurukshetra, Vol. 44, No. 3, December, 1995.

Castle, R., Chaudhari, D.P. and Nyland, C., "Child Labour in South Asia: Domestic and International Initiatives including ILO and WTO," Indian Journal of Labour Economics, Vol. 45, No. 3, July-September, 2002.

"Central Aid Sought to End Child Labour", The Hindu, 29 April, 1995.

"Centre urged to Enforce Child Labour Laws", The Hindu, 20 December, 1996.

"Centre's Scheme to Educate Child Labourers", The Hindu, 20 September, 1995.

Chanda, Rupa, "Child Labour and International Trade: Overview and Implications", Social Change, Vol. 27, Nos. 3-4, September-December, 1997.

Chandra, K. Suman, "Problems and Issues on Child Labour in India", Social Change, Vol. 27, Nos. 3-4, September-December, 1997.

Chandrasekhar, C.P., "The Economic Consequences of the Abolition of Child Labour: An Indian Case Study," Journal of Peasant Studies, Vol. 24, No. 3, April, 1997.

Chaudhri, D.D. and Nyland, Chris, "Globalisation, Demographic Pressures and Child Labour Standards," Indian Journal of Labour Economics, Vol. 45, No. 3, July-September, 2002.

Chaudhri, D.P., "Child Labour in India in the Asian Perspective 1951-96", Social Change, Vol. 27, Nos. 3-4, September-December, 1997.

Chaudhri, D.P., "Female Child Labour and Gender Bias in School Education in Indian States, 1961-91," The Indian Journal of Labour Economics, Vol. 40, No. 3, 1997.

"Child Labour abolition figures at Ministers Meet", The Hindu, 31 December, 1996.

"Child Labour and Adolescent Health," Health for the Millions, Vol. 21, No. 3, May-June, 1995.

"Child Labour," Awards Digest: Journal of Labour Legislation, Vol. XX, Nos. 7-12, July-December, 1994.

"Child Labour: Dimensions and Policy Options," Indian Journal of Labour Economics, Vol. 45, No. 3, July-September, 2002.

"Child Labour: Government to Conduct Surveys," The Hindu, 10 June, 1995.

"Child Labour in Carpet Industry," Margin, Vol. 27, No. 1, October-December, 1994.

"Child Labour in India", Social Change, Vol. 27, Nos. 3-4, September-December, 1997.

"Child Labour in Rich Countries too: UNICEF", The Hindu, 27 December, 1996.

"Child Labour Law and Practice," Conditions of Work Digest, Vol. X, No. 27, 1991.

"Child Labour Persists Despite Awareness", The Hindu, 29 October, 1996.

"Child Labour: Remedy can be worse than the Malady," The Hindu, 24 May, 1995.

"Child Labour, Removal to come under DGET," The Hindu, 5 November, 1994.

"Child Labour, SC gives Centre time to Reply", The Hindu, 20 February, 1996.

"Children of a Lesser God", Sunday Magazine, 12 January, 1997.

Dasgupta, Saibal, "No Child's Play," Business Standard, 4 February, 1997.

"Deadline suggested for ending Child Labour", The Hindu, 13 December, 1994.

Diamond, Charles and Fayed, Tammy, "Evidence on Substitutability of Adult and Child Labour", Journal of Development Studies, Vol. 34, No. 3, February, 1998.

"Double-Speak on Child Labour", The Hindu, 12 December, 1994.

Doval, N.K., "Double-speak on Child Labour", The Hindu, 28 December, 1994.

Dutta, Mahva, "Child Labour: A curse in the society", Young Indian, Vol. 12, No. 43, 25 May, 2002.

Dwarakanath, H.D., "Child Labour: Need for new Social Revolution", Kurukshetra, Vol. 47, No. 6, March, 1999.

"Economy is only one Dimension of Child Labour," The Hindu, 18 February, 1997.

"Eliminating the Child Labour" (a special feature), Yojana, Vol. 40, No. 5, May, 1996.

"Eradicating Child Labour is a Priority," The Hindu, 30 September, 1998.

Fernandes, Walter, "Child Labour and the Process of Exploitation," The Indian Journal of Social Work, Vol. LIII, No. 2, April, 1992.

"Focus on Child Labour" (a special feature), Kurukshetra, Vol. 39, No. 2, November, 1990.

"Focus on Elimination of Child Labour", The Hindu, 14 November, 1996.

"Focus on Eradicating Child Labour," The Hindu, 6 December, 1994.

Gopal, J. Nanda, "Child Labour", Hindu (Business Line), 19 March, 1996.

"Government Committed to Eradicating Child Labour", The Hindu, 25 January, 1998.

"Government Servants have failed to curb Child Employment," The Hindu, 11 August, 1995.

Gupta, Dipankar, "Child's Labour Lost", Telegraph, 15 January, 1999.

Gurumoorthy, T.R., "Child Labour — an Economic Issue", Third Concept, Vol. 10, Nos. 110-11, April-May, 1996.

Hamsa, "Tackling the Problem of Child Labour", Yojana, Vol. 32, No. 23, 1988.

Hanumantha Rao, K. and Madhusudhana Rao, M., "Employers's view of Child Labour", Indian Journal of Industrial Relations, Vol. 34, No. 1, July, 1998.

Hyder, S. Nazre, "Child Labour in Pakistan: Problems, Policies and Programmes", Asian Pacific Development Journal, Vol. 5, No. 1, June, 1998.

International Labour Office, "Employment Prospects of Children and Young People in Asia," International Labour Review, Vol. 88, 1963.

International Labour Review, Vol. 136, No. 2, ILO Office, Geneva, 1997.

Jain, Mahaveer, "Child Labour: Causes and Combat Strategies", Health for the Millions, Vol. 22, No. 1, January — February, 1996.

Joshi, Uma, "Lost Joys of Childhood", Social Welfare, Vol. 46, No. 8, November, 1999.

Joshi, Uma, "Restoring Childhood to Child Labour," Social Welfare, Vol. 44, No. 1, April, 1997.

Kaldate, Sudha, "Restoring Childhood Rights to Child Labour," Social Change, Vol. 27, Nos. 3-4, September-December, 1997.

Kapoor, H.L., "Child Labour: More Stringent Laws Needed," Statesman, 14 December, 1996.

Karunanithi, G., "Child Labour in Melapalayam, Social Welfare", Vol. 36, Nos. 10-11, January-February, 1990.

Kasbekar, S.R. and Samata, Dhawade, "Looking Beyond obvious alibis for Child Labour", Business Standard, 11 July, 1997.

Kaur, Kuldip and Kaur, Amandeep, "Child Labour in India: Causes and Implications", Anvesak, Vol. 32, No. 2, July-December, 2002.

Kaushik, Susheela, "Child Labour — Challenges and Opportunities", Social Welfare, Vol. 43, No. 1, April, 1996.

Krishnaji, N., "Working mothers and Child Survival in Rural India: Insights from Spatial Patterns", Economic and Political Weekly, Vol. 30, No. 44, 4 November, 1995.

Kumar, Hajira, "The Working Child: Wasted Childhood, Lost Youth," Social Welfare, Vol. 16, No. 7, October, 1999.

Kumar, Mohan, "Child Labourers Rescued by Mukti Ashram," Social Welfare, Vol. 43, No. 12, March, 1997.

Lal, Geeta, "Child Labour in India: An Overview", Social Change, Vol. 27, Nos. 3-4, September-December, 1997.

Lal, Manjula, "Under the Carpet", Pioneer, 13 May, 1999.

Laskar, Baharul Islam, "Child Labour in Aligarh Lock Industry", Economic and Political Weekly, Vol. 35, No. 7, 12 February, 2000.

Madhav, Ashok, "UNICEF's Strategy to Achieve Rights of Children", Trinity Mirror, Vol. 29, April, 1996.

Madhok, Alaka, "Child Labour: Some issues, some suggestions," Yojana, Vol. 40, No. 5, May, 1996.

Mahapatra, Sevashree, "Step to check Child Labour", Yojana, Vol. 41, No. 7, July, 1997.

Maharatna, Arup, "Children's Work Activities, Surplus Labour and Fertility: Case Study of Six Villages in Birbhum", Economic and Political Weekly, Vol. 32, No. 7, 15 February, 1997.

Majumdar, Bhaskar, "Why should a Child Labour"?, Young Indian, Vol. 10, No. 30, 4 March, 2000.

Manimekalai, N. and Kunjammal, R., "Ragpickers of Pendukkottai", Social Welfare, Vol. 46, No. 8, November, 1999.

Mehendale, Archana, "Law and Child Labour: A Case for Protecting Children's Rights", Social Change, Vol. 27, Nos. 3-4, September-December, 1997.

Mehta, Pradeep S., "Child Labour: Social Clause and the WTO", Economic Times, 16 June, 1999.

Mendelievich, Ellias, "Children at Work", International Labour Review, Vol. 118, No. 5, September-October, 1979.

Mishra, Lakshmidhar, "Three Approaches to Child Labour", Social Change, Vol. 27, Nos. 3-4, September-December, 1997.

Mittal, L.N., "Child Labour: Cure Lies in Spread of Education", Statesman, 30 May, 1997.

Mohanti, Neeti, "Gender Perspective in Child Labour", Social Welfare, Vol. 44, No. 1, April, 1997.

Mohsin, Nadeen, "Poverty, Breeding Ground of Child Labour", Mainstream, Vol. 18, No. 41, 1980.

Murthy, G.K. and Rani, T.J., "Wages of Child Labour", Yojana, Vol. 27, No. 18, 1983.

Naidu, A.N., "Child Labour Participation in India — A state wise Census Analysis", Journal of Family Welfare, Vol. XXVII, No. 4, June, 1981.

Narayana, K.S. and Rani, P. Pushpa, "Dimensions of Child Labour in Silk Industry — A Diagnostic Exercise", Young Indian, Vol. 10, No. 26, 5 February, 2000.

Nayar, Kuldip, "The Bane of Child Labour," Hindu, 20 December, 1997.

"New global estimates on Child Labour", Indian Journal of Labour Economics, Vol. 45, No. 3, July-September, 2002.

Panagariya, Arvind, "Curbing Child Labour: Rugmark Label on the Mat", Times of India, 14 November, 1996.

"Panel Pulls up Labour Ministry", Indian Express, 8 May, 1995.

"Panel to Monitor end Child Labour Project", The Hindu, 5 February, 1997.

Panigrahi, D.K., "Child Labour in India: An Overview", Social Change, Vol. 27, Nos. 3-4, September-December, 1997.

Parmar, M.N. and Solanki, Jagdish, "Girl Child Labour", Social Change, Vol. 27, Nos. 3-4, September-December, 1997.

Patil, Balagouda S., "Child Labour: Paradox for Social Scientists", Social Welfare, Vol. 46, No. 5, August, 1999.

Patil, Balagouda S., "Futility of Relying on Child Labour Legislation: Multiple Policy Approach Needed", Deccan Herald, 21 August, 1998.

Patil, B.R., "Eliminating Child Labour: Some National and International Initiatives," Social Change, Vol. 27, Nos. 3-4, September-December, 1997.

Patnam, Visala N. and Bhalerao, Alka R., "Child Labour — jobs that children do," Social Welfare, Vol. 43, No. 8, November, 1996.

Pattnaik, Satyanarayana and Bedi, Daljit Singh, "The Menace of Child Labour — Need for an Integrated Approach," Kurukshetra, Vol. 47, No. 3, December, 1998.

Perveen, Alfreen, "Some Social Problems of Child Labour: A Critical Analysis," Third Concept, Vol. 15, No. 74, August, 2001.

"Plan to Eradicate Child Labour", The Hindu, 9 June, 1995.

"PM wants time-bound end to Child Labour", The Hindu, 15 September, 1995.

Prasad, Narendra, "Child Labour in India," Yojana, Vol. 34, No. 8, 1 May, 1990.

"Problem of Child Labour Genuine", The Hindu, 10 May, 1995.

"Programme on Transit Schools for Child Labourers," The Hindu, 4 August, 1998.

"Projects Proposed to Eliminate Child Labour," The Hindu, 8 December, 1994

Punalekar, S.P., "Labouring Children: On Social Roots of Child Exploitation", Social Change, Vol. 27, Nos. 3-4, September-December, 1997.

Rajamani, Lavanyya, "Exploding the Myths about Child Labour", Journal of the Indian Law Institute, Vol. 37, No. 2, April- June, 1995.

Ramdoss, S., "Exploitation of Children", Third Concept, Vol. 16, No. 190, December, 2002.

"Rehabilitation Schemes for Child Labour", The Hindu, 26 July, 1996.

Remington, Francoise, "Child Labour: A Global Crisis without a Global Response", Economic and Political Weekly, Vol. 31, No. 52, 28 December, 1996.

"Residential Camp for Child Labourers", The Hindu, 25 May, 1998.

Rodgers, G. and Standing, G., "Economic Roles of Children in Low-Income Countries", International Labour Review, January-February, 1981.

Roy, Dunu, "Rights of Child Labour: Ethics, Production and Nation-State," Economic and Political Weekly, Vol. 33, No. 5, 31 January — 6 February, 1998.

Roy, Sunil C., "Child Labour: Eradicating the Evil", Yojana, Vol. 40, No. 1, January, 1996.

Rustagi, Preet, "Girl Child Labour: Regional dimensions and

motivations," Indian Journal of Labour Economics, Vol. 45, No. 3, July-September, 2002.

Sachchidananda, "Voluntary Agencies and Challenge of Eighties", Journal of Social and Economic Studies, Vol. IX, No. 2, 1981.

Sahay, K.B., "Child Labour: Where schooling is not Available", Statesman, 11 December, 1996.

Sambandan, V.S., "Bread winners at a Tender Age", The Hindu, 3 February, 1997.

Satyarthi, Kailash, "The Exploitation of Children in Carpet Industry", Health for the Millions, Vol. 21, No. 3, May-June, 1995.

Saxena, Archana, "Eliminating Child Labour Needs a Collective Approach", Social Welfare, Vol. 46, No. 8, November, 1999.

"SC ban renders Children Jobless", The Hindu, 7 May, 1997.

"Scheme to Rehabilitate Child Labour", The Hindu, 5 August, 1995.

Sharma, Kalpana, "Why should children Work"?, The Hindu, 20 December, 1996.

Sharma, K.S., "Combating Child Labour: Empowerment of Parents and Child Workers", Third Concept, Vol. 11, Nos. 122-23, April-May, 1997.

Siddiqi, Z.M. Shahid, "Enforcement of Child Labour Laws", Mainstream, Vol. 37, No. 18, 24 April, 1999.

Sikligar, P.C., "Child Labour: A Sociological Analysis and its Implications", Anvesak, Vol. 28, No. 2, July-December, 1998.

Singh, A.N., "Problems confronting Child Ragpickers in Slums", Indian Journal of Social Work, Vol. 60, No. 2, April 1999.

Singh, Om Raj, "Childhood Sans Innocence", Social Welfare, Vol. 46, No. 8, November, 1999.

Singh, Sahib, "Child Labour problems and possible solutions", Yojana, Vol. 47, No. 5, May, 2003.

Singh, S.P., "Child Labour: The malady and the remedy", Yojana, Vol. 41, No. 7, July, 1997.

Sinha, Shantha, "Child Labour and Education," Seminar, Vol. 474, February 1999.

"Slum Board to eliminate Child Labour", The Hindu, 22 November, 1995.

"Special issue on Child Labour", Awards Digest:Journal of Labour Legislation, Vol. XVII, Nos. 3-6, March-June, 1993.

"Special issue on Child Labour and Education", Administrator, Vol. 41, No. 3, July-September, 1996.

"Special issue on Child Labour", NLI News Letter, Vol. 3, Nos. 3-4, August-September, 1995.

"Special issue on Education of Working Children," Journal of Educational Planning and Administration, Vol. 4, No. 1, January, 1990.

Srivastava, Sushila and Bhanumathi, R., "Child Workers in Farming, Domestic and Catering Sectors," Social Welfare, Vol. 37, No. 7, October, 1990.

"Street Play's role in ending Child Labour Stressed," The Hindu, 28 January, 1997.

Tanwar, Reicha, "Female Child Labour and Education in Haryana," Social Change, Vol. 27, Nos. 3-4, September-December, 1997.

Times of India, July 21, 1998.

Tiwari, Arvind, "Child Labour in India: Ways and Means to Tackle the Malady," Social Change, Vol. 27, Nos. 3-4, September-December, 1997.

"To the girl child her due", The Hindu, 25 March, 1998.

"UNICEF call to Eliminate hazardous Child Labour", The Hindu, 11 December, 1997.

Verma, A.K. "Child Labour in India", Manpower Journal, Vol. XXI, No. 1, April-June, 1985.

Verma, Suman, "The working children in India", Child Worker in Asia, Vol. 10, No. 3, July-September, 1994.

Verma, V., "Child Labour Need for Social Awareness", in Yojana, Vol. 23, No. 2, 1979.

Viswanathan, P., "Child Labour in India", The Economic Times, 10 April, 1982.

Vittal, N., "A New approach to Child Labour", Economic Times, 10 March, 1988.

Vora, Alpa, Kamat, Madhuri and Rao, Suresh, "Child Labour — Awaiting the exit Policy", Social Change, Vol. 27, Nos. 3-4, September-December, 1997.

Wazir, Rekha, "Eliminating Child Labour: Do NGO interventions add up to a strategy? "Indian Journal of Labour Economics, Vol. 45, No. 3, July-September, 2002.

Wazir, Rekha, "No to Child Labour, yes to Education: Unfolding of a grass roots movement in Andhra Pradesh, "Economic and Political Weekly, Vol. 37, No. 52, 28 December, 2002.

Weiner, Myron, "Child Labour in India: Putting compulsory primary Education on the Political Agenda", Economic and Political Weekly, Vol. 31, Nos. 45-46, 9 November, 1996.

"West must share cost of Child Labour Abolition", The Hindu, 14 June, 1995.

"West not competent to Preach on Child Labour", The Hindu, 14 December, 1997.

"What the Children say", The Hindu, 2 February, 1997.

"When will they say goodbye to workspots?", The Hindu, 30 April, 1996.

Yojurvedi, V.P., "Convergence and elimination of Child Labour", Yojana, Vol. 46, November, 2002.

Annexure

Questionnaire for Working Children

1. Name :
2. Age :
3. Place of stay :
4. Native of which place :
5. Gender : Male/Female
6. What kind of family do you belong?
   i) Joint
   ii) Nuclear
   iii) Extended
   iv) Single Parent
7. How many members are there in your family?
   i) 1-4
   ii) 4-8
   iii) 8-12
8. How many brothers and sisters you have?
   i) Brothers :
   ii) Sisters :
9. How many of you are engaged in one or the other occupation?
10. Whether any of your brothers/sisters are engaged in rag picking work? Yes/No
    If yes, how much he/she earns out of that?
11. Where does your family live?
    i) Own house
    ii) Rented house
    iii) Jhugi Jhopari
12. What is the space in the house?
    i) one room including kitchen
    ii) one room plus kitchen
    iii) two rooms plus kitchen
13. Profession of father :
14. Profession of mother :

15. Addiction of Guardian
    - i) Drinking
    - ii) Smoking
    - iii) Drugs
    - iv) None
16. Whether you have some addiction?Yes/No
    - i) If yes, of what type?
    - ii) Since how long?
17. What led to you to work as a child labour?
    - i) Broken family
    - ii) Alcoholic Parents
    - iii) Lack of Parental care
    - iv) Low interest in studies
    - v) Pressure from parents
    - vi) Illiteracy among parents
    - vii) To supplement family income
    - viii) For better living

18) Your educational qualification:
    - i) Primary
    - ii) Secondary
    - iii) Uneducated

19. Whether you are a drop out? Yes/No

    If yes, please assign reasons for being drop out.
    - i) Family condition
    - ii) Lack of school facilities
    - iii) Motive of earning for the family
    - iv) Motive to get pocket money for personal use
    - v) Under the influence of friends
    - vi) Any other
20. Do you think that work is more important than education?Yes/No

    If yes, why do you think so?
    - i) To earn money
    - ii) Not interested in studies
    - iii) No earning member in the family
    - iv) To supplement family's income
    - v) Family environment
    - vi) To learn the work
    - viii) Parents compulsion

21. Are you interested in studying?
    i) Full time
    ii) Non-formal education
    iii) Not at all
22. In what occupation you are engaged?
    i)
    ii)
    iii)
    iv)
23. What is the mode of payment?
    i) Daily Wage
    ii) Weekly Payment
    iii) Monthly Salary
24. How much you earn in a month?
    i) 300-500
    ii) 500-700
    iii) 700-1000
25. How much you contribute to your family?
26. How much you spend on yourself?
27. In which place/area do you work?
28. How far is the distance between the place of work and your residence?
    i) Very near
    ii) Short distance
    iii) Long distance
29. At which age did you start working?
30. Whether this is your first job? Yes/No
    If yes, please explain the working condition.
31. How long have you been doing this present work?
32. How many hours do you work daily?
33. How long you remain out of your house?
34. What do you do during your spare time?
    i) Play
    ii) Rest
    iii) Watch movie
    iv) Study
    v) Do some other work
35. Do you get any rest interval other than lunch break? Yes/No
36. Do you get weekly holidays? Yes/No

37. Is there a cut in your wages if you take leave? Yes/No
38. Do you work overtime? Yes/No
    If yes, are you paid for overtime work?
39. Are you made to work even at the time of festivals? Yes/No
    If yes, are you paid for it?
40. What all facilities are lacking at your workplace?
    i) Spacious rooms
    ii) Proper ventilation
    iii) Safe drinking water
    iv) Toilets
    v) Sunlight
41. Other than salary, what extra benefits do you get?
    i) Medical care
    ii) Transport facility
    iii) Food
    iv) House
    v) None
42. How does your employer treat you?
    i) Beating
    ii) Scolding
    iii) Not giving salary
    iv) None
43. Does your employer listen to your grievances?
    i) Sometimes
    ii) Always
    iii) Never
    iv) Rarely
44. Are you satisfied with your job? Yes/No
    If yes, to what extent?
    i) Very much
    ii) Somewhat
    iii) Not at all
45. Some organized gangs use the children of your age group for pick pocketing. Are you aware of them? Yes/No
    i) If yes, whether you were at any point of time engaged in that? Yes/No
    ii) If yes, what used to be the share of earning between you and the gang?

46. Whether you were caught pick pocketing by the police? Yes/No
    If yes, whether you were put in remand home or left free by the police?
47. Some people engage children of your age group for immoral traffic. Are you aware of this? Yes/No
    If yes, whether you have fallen in such trap?
48. What is your future plan?
    i) To remain in the same work
    ii) To join some other work
    iii) Quit the work and start studying
    iv) To get technical training
    v) Whatever parent's say
    v) Do not know.

Index